ISRAEL ACT III

by
Richard Wolff

Tyndale House, Publishers, Wheaton, Illinois

"I will restore the fortunes of my people Israel, and they shall rebuild their ruined cities, and live in them again; and they shall plant vineyards and gardens and eat their crops and drink their wine.

I will firmly plant them there upon the land that I have given them; they shall not be pulled up again, says the Lord your God."

(Amos 9:14-15, *Living Prophecies*)

CONTENTS

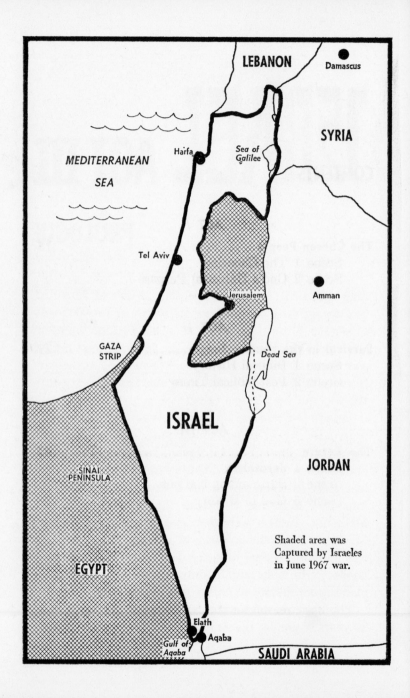

ISRAEL ACT III

PROLOGUE

On Monday, June 5, 1967, in stunning predawn air strikes, the tiny nation of Israel all but annihilated the massed air forces of hostile Arab countries. Within hours the 25 most vital air bases in the Arab world had been wrecked. In four hours the air war against Nasser was won. In 60 hours the Jordanian, Syrian and Iraqi air forces were shattered. In six days the war was over. Some called it a mini-war.

Israel's Mystere and Mirage jets, made in France, neatly avoided Egypt's Soviet-built radar defense network. Egyptian radar was aimed toward Israel but the Israeli planes came across the Mediterranean. Flying at 500 feet, they slammed new secret 12-foot directional bombs into 200 front-line Egyptian fighter planes, mostly MIG-21's. Bombs were not even wasted on dummy MIGs placed on the air strips as decoys. This selectivity was possible because of a new Israeli device for homing bombs onto live targets only. Literally hundreds of planes were destroyed on the ground.

The basic reason for the Israeli-Arab third conflict in 20 years is simple: the Arab nations have not recognized the right of Israel to exist. "For twenty years, hatred of Israel has been the whiskey of the Arabs—and the Middle East will not be stable or safe until they are off the stuff,"[1] says a *Life* magazine writer. This hatred had inspired increasing terrorism, especially on the Syrian border. On May 18, 1967, the U.N. peace force stopped patrolling the Gaza Strip border with Israel at the request of Egypt's President Nasser. The U.N. Expeditionary Force had been stationed on the Egyptian side of the border ever since the hostilities of 1956. Nasser had talked a great deal about the coming liberation struggle, but the U.N. "pane of glass" prevented Egypt from decisive action. To demonstrate that he meant to match words with deeds, Nasser asked the U.N.E.F. to withdraw. Egypt was now in a position to deter Israel from action against Syria.

On May 22 Nasser blockaded the Gulf of Aqaba and declared: "We are ready for war." Before the Suez Campaign of 1956 Egypt had refused passage through the Gulf to Israeli vessels seeking to reach the port of Elath. After the 1956 campaign the U.N. placed a garrison at Sharm el Sheikh. The dismissal of U.N. forces cleared the way for a new blockade. This was critical because the port of Elath handled almost 90 percent of Israel's vital oil supplies arriving from Iran, as well as the large Israeli trade with East Africa, India and the East.

On May 30 the noose tightened. President Nasser patched up his feud with King Hussein of Jordan and signed a military pact. Israel, encircled as the stage was set, had the odds heavily against her. Egypt moved 80,000 troops into the Gaza Strip. Russian-built missiles and giant rockets and 900 tanks were pointing at

[1] *Life*, June 16, 1967, Page 4.

Israel. On the northern border 40,000 Syrians, rein-
forced by 5,000 Iraqi soldiers were ready to strike. On
the east side 40,000 Jordanians were prepared to resume
hostilities. Saudi Arabia had ordered 20,000 men into
Jordan. Israel faced the hostility of 14 Arab nations representing 110 million people. Israel's regular army to-
talled only 70,000 men, but a splendid system enabled
them to organize 230,000 reserves, about half the total
male population of military age.

The presence of Russian warships in the Mediterranean caused considerable concern. It was known that
Russian missiles with a twenty-four mile range had been
installed in the Sinai within range of the Israeli Nuclear
Center near Beersheba. Later nine were captured intact,
with carriers cocked for action. It was also known that
German scientists had been working in Egypt for years
to build liquid fuel rockets. Egypt was in possession of
ground-to-ground "al Kahir" and "al Zafir" rockets.
Worse, 350 Israeli warplanes faced 800 high perform-
ance enemy jets. Israel had developed a special guided
bomb and the air force was in superb condition. The
new and secret 12-foot directional bombs were most
effective.

It was generally recognized in Israel that the war
would have to be won within ten days. Otherwise the
immense numerical superiority of the Arabs would ultimately overcome the Israeli army. In addition, dwind-
ling fuel reserves would have quickly been exhausted.
Economically, Israel was not able to maintain a lengthy
defensive posture or she would go bankrupt. The whole
country became an armed camp; Arab pressure and
propaganda threatening annihilation left no other
choice. To remain in this position would have crippled

Israeli economy and ruined the nation. Under these circumstances the question: Who fired the first shot? becomes academic.

Aggressive Arab intentions were later confirmed by captured documents. Israel called the Egyptian blockade an act of aggression. The war moved swiftly. In spite of numerical inferiority, Israel achieved her basic objectives with astonishing suddenness: to occupy the Gaza Strip, Old Jerusalem, the Straits of Tiran, the west bank of the Jordan, the Syrian border heights—and to reach the Suez Canal.

Through control of the skies, victory was achieved by Wednesday, June 7, 1967. Summarized the *Chicago Daily News:* "The third day of the war was the Arab world's Waterloo, Dunkirk and Bay of Pigs all rolled into one. Israel smashed through to the Suez Canal on one front. It secured the old city of Jerusalem and won back the Wailing Wall, most sacred site in Judaism. Paratroops took Sharm el Sheikh at the Tiran Straits, freeing Aqaba. Armor rolled to the banks of the Jordan, capturing Bethlehem and Jericho and erasing the Jordanian bulge in Israel's silhouette."[2] Six days after the opening of the hostilities, the Israelis had captured nine Egyptian generals and ten colonels. Death casualties were high: 2,000 Syrians, 8,000 Jordanians, perhaps as many as 20,000 Egyptians and 679 Israelis. The cost of the war was estimated at $100 million for Israel over against $1,500,000,000 for the Arab nations.

The economic life of Israel had hardly been disrupted. Israel with a total working force of about 900,000 men and women had called 200,000 of these into military service during the war. Within days many were back at

[2]*Chicago Daily News*, June 20, 1967.

their old jobs. The nation's exports for June were almost normal. Officials hoped aloud that the previous hurdle in attracting foreign capital—the constant threat of war with the Arabs—had now been removed. An inflow of foreign capital was expected. Officials also expected a tremendous boom of tourism as a result of the war because of renewed interest in Israel. Besides, Israel controlled the entire city of Jerusalem and had at least temporary control of the Sinai oil wells which produce enough oil to meet all the needs of Israel. Some of these economic gains may be lost again.

Unemployment had been a significant problem in Israel. More than ten percent of the labor force needed jobs. This was the first significant setback since 1948. The number of Jewish immigrants fell to 12,000 in 1966 and the gross national product rose only by a fraction—1.6 percent—barely enough to compensate for the natural growth in population. It had seemed that the economic miracle might be at an end.

Immediately after the six-day war, Rachel Ben Zvi, widow of Israel's second president, said: "We badly need people. We need at least a million. We need people of all kinds: teachers, intellectual people, people to establish factories, technicians, builders, students, each to live and work in his own way. We need people of all ages. I believe they will come. Today we have no limit to our opportunities."[3]

On the other side, Egypt suffered economic disaster. Over the last ten years they had received $2 billion worth of Russian jets, tanks and guns. Most of this war materiel was destroyed. On June 26 it was reported that disaster threatened Egypt's cotton, the most important

[3]*Chicago Tribune,* June 22, 1967.

factor in their economy. A large scale leaf worm infestation was threatening the cotton crop—worst in 15 years. Egypt conceded that stocks of insecticide were exhausted. The economy also suffered serious blows from the closing of the Suez Canal and the slump in foreign tourism, the two other main sources of hard currency.

Israel undoubtedly has no less than three important goals: to establish Israel's legal existence and its territorial integrity; to provide for guarantees against maritime blockades; to insure freedom of passage in the Gulf of Aqaba and the Suez Canal. Israel would also like to retain Old Jerusalem. The reasons are deeper than strategy or security. Any government leader who returned this section of Jerusalem to Jordan would undoubtedly be expelled. The ultimate decision is difficult to foresee.

Most significant from a Christian standpoint are the spiritual and religious implications. "All over the country" wrote newsman William Stephenson, "the more orthodox Jews were talking of a new Messiah heralded by the return to the wall. Many believed he would appear on Wednesday, June 14, the festival of the giving of the Torah *(Shavuot)*, the traditional birthday and death anniversary of King David. On that day thousands of Jews walked along the four and one-half kilometers to Mt. Zion through the Dung Gate, and back through the Armenian quarter to Jaffa Gate. Mothers pushed children in prams and youths supported gray-bearded parents come to take a last look at the wall that they had never before seen. Hundreds spent all night around Mt. Zion, praying.[4]

A closing chapter in the book just quoted was written by Leon Uris, author of *Exodus*. His last lines are: "And

[4]*Strike Zion,* Wm. Stephenson, Bantam Books, 1967, page 75-76.

they stood before the western wall of the temple and prayed and danced and they wept for joy. And the Lord felt they had kept the faith well and suffered enough. And he bade them build a third temple and dwell in their own land forever."[5]

Time Magazine of June 30, 1967 raised the question: "Should the temple be rebuilt?" Obstacles are mentioned, especially the fact that the temple should be administered by priests. At this point it is impossible to trace authentic genealogies and to discover who belongs to the family of the priests. The animal sacrifices are part and parcel of the temple service and yet they would be "alien to the humane sensitivities of most modern Jews". Further discussion on the reconstruction of the temple in relation to Biblical truth will appear in subsequent pages of this book.

Although the immediate reasons for the new conflict can be traced back to early 1967, it can also be said that the basic reasons for current strife go back centuries to Isaac and Ishmael, or to God's call of Abraham. In order to gain a proper understanding of the present Mideast situation, a review of biblical concepts regarding Israel is necessary.

Bible readers say the significance of Israel's military victory is its renewed evidence that the God of Israel still lives, that his promises of protection and guidance will be fulfilled, and that the establishment of a strong Israel ushers in Act III on the stage of world history, a history that will end as Jesus Christ returns to establish peace and justice for humanity. The real-life drama of the Jews and human redemption began 40 centuries ago with a man named Abraham . . .

[5]Ibid, page 142.

13

ACT I

THE CHOSEN PEOPLE

You may recall the old epigram:

How odd
Of God
To choose
The Jews.

At times you may have shared the same feeling. Why did God select this people? It is true, of course, that if he had chosen any other nation, the same question would have been raised. In other words, why choose any nation at all? Does not God's concern extend over all nations? Is he not the God of the whole world?

Scene 1

The Choosing

The Bible makes it crystal clear that the Jews are the "Chosen People." The fact of national election or choice is stressed again and again: "The Lord has chosen you to be a people for his own possession, out of all the peoples that are on the face of the earth . . . The Lord has chosen Jacob for himself, Israel as his own possession." (Deut. 14:2; Ps. 135:4)

God's choice is also expressed by the simple expression "to know." God had chosen Abraham, literally "known" him. (Gen. 18:19) The prophet Amos announces: "You only have I known of all the families of the earth." (3:2) The word *to know* is descriptive of an intimate relationship, of personal knowledge, of a genuine concern. It describes a knowledge based on love. The word is used for the most intimate human relationships; we read that Adam knew Eve, his wife, and she conceived. Jesus said: "I know my own and my own know me, as the Father knows me and I know the Father." (John 10:14) He then adds: "I lay down my life for the sheep."

The knowledge he refers to designates a unique relationship rooted in love, and the divine choice of Israel is based on the sovereign love of God. This is confirmed by the words of Moses: "Behold, to the Lord your God belong heaven and the heaven of heavens, the earth with all that is in it; yet the Lord set his heart in love upon your fathers and chose their descendants after them, you above all peoples, as at this day." (Deut. 10:14, 15)

This love of God, manifesting itself in election, is unconditional and is not based upon any particular quality in the nation. "God has chosen you to be a people for his own possession, out of all the peoples that are on the face of the earth. It was not because you were more in number than any other people that the Lord set his love upon you and chose you, for you were the fewest of all people." (Deut. 7:6, 7) As a matter of fact, Israel is frequently called a stubborn people devoid of righteousness, yet chosen unconditionally and for eternal purposes.

Some people have suggested that the Jewish people were chosen because the Semitic people as a whole are distinguished by a genius for religion. It is suggested that Israel had attained an advanced stage of religious understanding, fitting them particularly for divine election. Even if this were true, it would still not explain why Israel was chosen, for the Semitic family would certainly include the Arabs, along with people of several other nations.

A look at Bible history shows that this thesis is totally contrary to fact. In spite of the divine revelation, Israel fell into idolatry, and regardless of the divine admonition persisted in the rejection of God. This is all the more remarkable because, as Jeremiah puts it: "Look around you and see if you can find another nation anywhere that has traded in its old gods for new ones—even though their gods are nothing. Send to the west, to the island of Cyprus; send to the east, to the deserts of Kedar. See if anyone there has heard so strange a thing as this. And yet my people have given up their glorious God for silly idols!" (2:10, 11)

Israel's persistent rejection of God in favor of idols ultimately led to the Babylonian captivity. The God of their fathers persistently sent to them his messengers, because he had compassion on his people, but they kept mocking the messengers of God, despising his words, scoffing at his prophets, until the wrath of the Lord rose against his people, until there was no remedy. God brought up against them the king of the Chaldeans and gave Jerusalem and the temple over to total destruction. The report of the chronicler is an apt summary of the history of the Jewish nation up to that time. (II Chron. 36:15 ff.) Far from showing religious genius, Israel illustrates the incurable wickedness of mankind.

Scene 2

God's Universal Purpose

The purpose of the divine election of Israel was at least threefold: that through this nation the Saviour should come into the world, that Israel would be the depository of divine revelation, and that Israel should carry God's message to all nations.

Regarding the first, one of the immediate purposes of Israel's election was that they would be the nation to give birth to the promised Messiah. It is in this sense that salvation is of the Jews. (John 4:22) The initial word of God to Abraham was: "In thee shall all the families of the earth be blessed." (Gen. 12:3) It is explicitly stated, "In thy seed shall all the nations of the earth be blessed." (Gen. 22:18) That the ultimate fulfillment is in Christ needs no further amplification.

The promise narrowed in the choice between Abraham's grandsons. It was resolved by the action of Esau who sold his birthright to Jacob for a dish of red pottage. While this birthright involved the chieftainship, it involved most of all the blessing of Abraham, the unique covenant relationship with God. (Gen. 28:4) Esau despised the headship of the tribe both spiritual and temporal and the covenant blessing. Afterwards he tried to secure that which he had deliberately sold. Esau became the father of the Edomites who occupied the area between the Salt Sea and the Gulf of Aqaba and were bitter enemies of Israel throughout their history.

Jacob was far from blameless in his transaction with Esau, but the birthright stayed in his possession and the choice of Israel was confirmed. In due time, Christ was born of Mary, and later the apostle Paul, enumerating the privileges of Israel, mentions that Christ was a Jew as far as his human nature was concerned. (Rom. 9:5)

The Jews have sometimes been called the people of the Book. The psalmist celebrates the fact that God had declared his word to Jacob, his statutes and ordinances to Israel. He has not dealt thus with any other nations; they do not know his ordinances. (147:19, 20) Paul also stated that one of the outstanding advantages of the Jew was that the oracles of God had been entrusted to them. (Rom. 3:1, 2)

Their faithlessness and disobedience did not nullify the faithfulness of God. The Jewish people have both received and preserved the Scriptures. This is all the more remarkable because their infidelity is condemned by the very Scriptures they preserved. As Pascal observed:

"The law of the Jews is at the same time the severest and strictest of all in respect to their religious worship, imposing on this people, in order to keep them to their duty, a thousand peculiar and painful observances, on pain of death. Whence it is very astonishing that it has been constantly preserved during many centuries by a people, rebellious and impatient as this one was; while all other states have changed their laws from time to time, although these were far more lenient."[6]

Election is not primarily a privilege but a responsibility, a challenge and a calling. It is the irrevocable purpose of God that the earth shall be full of the knowledge of the Lord as the waters cover the sea. It is, therefore, to be expected that God would appoint Israel to be his witness among all nations. Israel is called God's son, his firstborn—an obvious indication that other nations also shall enter into the role of sonship. Again and again Israel is challenged to be the witness of God to all nations. (Exodus 4:22; Isaiah 43:11, 12, 21) Here, too, the divine purpose has been fulfilled.

Jewish Missionaries

In the past, the Jewish people have been active missionaries. The Babylonian exile brought them into personal contact with many nations. Their later enforced migrations created new contacts with pagan nations.

A concrete example is the relationship between Israel and Egypt. It is generally recognized that Jewish immigrants exerted a leavening influence upon Egypt. Sizeable Hebrew-speaking colonies were established in several Egyptian cities. A Jewish temple was built at Leontopolis by Onias IV, in the time of Ptolemy Philometor. For two centuries this temple shared with the temple of Jerusalem the homage of Egyptian Jews.

Under Ptolemy I, large numbers of Jewish immi-

---

[6]*Pensees*, Blaise Pascal, J. M. Dent and Sons, London, 1948, p. 174-175.

grants settled at Alexandria with full toleration of their faith and worship. Under Ptolemy Philadelphus, a constant relationship between the Palestinians and Egyptians led to the translation of the Old Testament Scriptures in what we know as the Septuagint. This, in turn, was followed by the growth of a Greco-Jewish literature of which we have the remains in the Apocrypha and the writings of Philo.

Even Jesus Christ referred to the extraordinary zeal of the Pharisees who traveled through land and sea to make a single proselyte. (Matt. 23:15) The Jewish historian Josephus writes: "The multitude of mankind itself has had a great inclination for a long time to follow our religious observances; for there is not any city of the Grecians nor any of the barbarians, nor any nation whatsoever, where our custom of resting on the seventh day has not come, and by which our fasts and lighting up lamps and many of our prohibitions as to our food, are not observed." Josephus also writes that many of the Greeks "have come over to our laws, and some of them have continued in their observation, although others of them had not courage enough to persevere and so departed from them again." (*Against Apion II*, 40/11)

The Book of Acts mentions the proselytes who were at Jerusalem on the day of Pentecost. (2:10) Many of these converts to Judaism became the nucleus of the Christian Church as they responded to the preaching of Paul. The Book of Acts refers to them as those "that fear God" and Paul reached them in Antioch of Pisidia, Athens, and other cities. (Acts 13:43 and 17:17) The kingdom of Adiapene, located between the Roman Empire and the Parthian Kingdom, were under Jewish influence when the queen embraced the Jewish religion.

Internal and external circumstances put an end to this missionary zeal. The government prohibited proselytizing and the Jewish tradition hardened in rabbinical interpretations that are preserved to this day in the *Talmud*. But regardless of the external or internal factors it is a historic fact that Jewish missionary zeal slackened and the Christian Church took over the tremendous missionary task of proclaiming the message of God to all nations.

As Israel was elected as a nation, the individual Christian knows himself to be chosen by God, elected to salvation and service, in missionary proclamation. This does not nullify the election of the Jewish people as a nation. They are still the chosen nation, selected for divine and sovereign purposes, but no longer in the active stream of history and fulfillment as far as the missionary calling is concerned. One might, perhaps, say that they have become negative or mute witnesses.

The Scriptures had predicted that the Jewish people would be scattered to the four corners of the world in case of disobedience. Such national rebellion took place, and the Jews have indeed been scattered throughout the earth. In that sense, every living Jew in every country of the world is a direct testimony to the truthfulness of the divine declaration. This mute and negative witness needs to be complemented by the positive and joyful witness of the Christian as he points to salvation in Christ. In the words of Paul, "Note then the kindness and severity of God: severity towards those who have fallen, but God's kindness to you, provided you continue in his kindness; otherwise you too will be cut off." (Rom. 11:22)

The sovereign power of God is illustrated in the election of Israel despite the failures of the Chosen People. It is true that the message of God through the prophets was rejected and the Babylonian exile resulted. It is also true that Christ came to his own people and they did not receive him. As the Jews had rejected the Father in Old Testament days, so their descendants now refused the Son. Finally they rejected the testimony of the Holy Spirit who addressed the nation through the apostles. Peter admonished Israel to repent and pleaded with them to turn to God so that their sins would be blotted out and "the times of refreshing" might come from the presence of the Lord.

The apostolic witness lasted for one whole generation but was rejected, and the nation was led into the dispersion which lasted for centuries. Jerusalem was destroyed by the Romans in A.D. 70, and the nation became homeless for centuries.

The revelation of the Father, the person of the Son, the message of the Holy Spirit had been rejected by the chosen nation. Election had not kept the nation from judgment. The Babylonian captivity lasted only 70 years and was limited in scope. The exile following the destruction of Jerusalem lasted for almost 2,000 years and was worldwide in its implications. In spite of persistent rebellion the purpose of divine election has been fulfilled—a striking illustration of the sovereignty of God in history.

A Tribal God?

God is never seen as a mere tribal or national deity in the Old Testament. Such a view would debase God to the stature of an idol and be a caricature of the true God. Throughout the Old Testament runs the proclamation that there is only one God. This truth requires necessarily that he is the God of all nations. No other God should be worshiped by any nation for there is none other. The God of Israel is the God of the whole world. Given the idea of monotheism, the missionary concept must necessarily follow. Jesus Christ was, of course, referring to the Old Testament when he told the disciples after his resurrection: "It is written that the Christ should suffer and on the third day arise from the dead, and that repentance and forgiveness of sins should be preached in his name to all nations." (Luke 24:25-47) The words "to all nations" are characteristic of the Old Testament as well as of the New Testament. The Great Commission is not an afterthought, but a formal summarization in the New Testament of the entire teaching of the Scriptures. The career of the prophet Jonah is not the isolated venture of an inspired Jew, but is characteristic of the missionary concern which should have dominated every true Israelite.

The election of Israel did not limit God's worldwide purposes to one single nation. On the contrary, this choice was a means to implement his grace and mercy toward all nations. Far from justifying narrow nationalism and pride, election is a call to service and responsibility.

In a striking passage Amos speaks God's words: "O people of Israel, are you any more to me than the Ethiopians are? Have not I, who brought you out of Egypt, done as much for other people too? I brought the Philistines from Caphtor and the Syrians out of Kir." (Amos 9:7)

The Israelites were only too ready to argue that God, after the marks of favor which he had bestowed on his people, would never cast them off, and that they were immune from judgment. The prophet reminds them that apart from God's choice, they had no more significance than any other nation. God did not only lead Israel out of Egypt, but he also directed the migrations of all other nations, even of those who were historically bitter enemies of Israel—even the remote Cushites (Ethiopians).

It is a temptation for anyone to believe that election implies privilege, not responsibility. Christians may feel that the blessing of God must automatically rest upon them. As a matter of fact, judgment begins at the house of God. Having said, "Of all the peoples of the earth, I have chosen you alone," the prophet Amos adds God's explanation: "This is why I must punish you the more for your sins." That the fact of election does not shield from judgment is certainly demonstrated throughout the history of Israel.

At the initial call of Abraham to follow him, God announced that *all* the families of the earth would be blessed. God announced that the earth will be filled with his glory (Num. 14:21), a promise ultimately realized through Jesus Christ, who is the "light of the Gentiles." (Isaiah 42.)

Monotheism is linked directly to worldwide missions in Scripture: "There is no other God besides me, a righteous God and a Saviour; there is none besides me. Come unto me and be saved, all the ends of the earth! For I am God and there is no other." (Isaiah 45:21, 22)

Similarly, the psalmist exclaims: "There is none like thee among the gods, O Lord, nor are there any works like thine. All the nations thou hast made shall come and bow down before thee, O Lord, and shall glorify thy name." (Ps. 86:8, 9) Psalm 96 echoes the same thought.

All the earth is admonished to sing unto God. Israel is challenged to declare his glory among the nations because all the gods of the peoples are idols, but the God of Israel is the Creator who made the heavens. Again and again this thought is found in the Old Testament poets and prophets. It is the Old Testament that first proclaimed that whosoever shall call on the name of the Lord shall be saved, and the very last book of the Old Testament announces: "From the rising of the sun even to the going down of the same my name shall be great among the Gentiles . . . My name shall be great among the heathen, saith the Lord of Hosts. (Malachi 1:11) When Jesus said that the field is the world, that God loved the world and that his Gospel must be preached among all nations, he was restating the promise that the redemptive and gracious purposes of God embrace the whole world.

After the Babylonian Exile of Israel, the people were largely cured of idolatry, but isolationists among them erected unnatural barriers and the nation as a whole lost sight of God's purpose. The Christian Church, called to be the light of the world, is correctly informed that Christ died for all. But theological accuracy has not produced corresponding action. The failures of the Jewish nation and of the Christian Church may have made God appear partial in his choice, but God's sovereign love has always embraced all men, Jew and Gentile, men of all nations and of all races.

ACT II

SURVIVAL IN THE HUMAN JUNGLE

When God called Abraham away from the city of Ur, he said: "Go from your country and your kindred and your father's house to the land that I will show you." Abraham reached the land of the Canaanites where God told him: "To your descendants I will give this land."

This promise was repeated several times and finally elaborated: "To your descendants I will give this land, from the river of Egypt to the great river, the river Euphrates." Abraham was assured that the land of Canaan would be given to his descendants for an everlasting possession. At the same time Israel was warned that in case of disobedience to God Israel would be defeated and exiled. (Deut. 28) The possession of the land was part of the Covenant.[7]

[7]Gen. 13:15; 15:18; 17:8; 24:7; 26:3; 28:4, 13; 35:12; 48:4.

Scene 1

Biblical History

It is remarkable that Israel was able to maintain its national identity even when they were in the Promised Land. By reason of its geographical position, Palestine was a buffer state between the great powers of the ancient world. The kingdom of Israel was exposed to influences which tended to destroy the individuality of national life. This became the fate of nation after nation surrounding the Jewish State. Most of the ancient tribes and kingdoms in that area have long since disappeared from the scene of history. Yet, although repeatedly subdued and oppressed by their conquerors for almost 2,000 years, Israel retained its identify.

Commenting on Israel's survival, historian Arnold Toynbee wrote: "As for long life, the Jews live on—the same peculiar people—today, long ages after the Phoenicians and the Philistines have lost their identity. Their ancient Syriac neighbors have gone into the melting-pot and have been reminted, with new images and superscriptions, while Israel has proved impervious to this alchemy—performed by history in the crucibles of universal states and universal churches and wanderings of the nations—to which we Gentiles all in turn succumb."[8]

Similarly, Will Durant writes: "One would not expect so tiny a territory to play a major role in history, or to leave behind an influence greater than that of Babylonia, Assyria, or Persia, perhaps greater than even that of Egypt or Greece. But it was the fortune and misfortune of Palestine that it lay midway between the capitals of the Nile and those of the Tigris and Euphrates. This circumstance brought trading to Judea, and it brought wars; time and again the harassed Hebrews were compelled to take sides in the struggle of the empires, or to pay tribute, or be overrun."[9]

But if the history of the Jews is remarkable in this respect, so long as they remained in their own land, it is much more so since they have been an exiled nation.

It may not be easy to define what constitutes a nation. There has to be a sense of common identity, a common tradition and a specific territory. It is remarkable that in spite of centuries of dispersion the Jews have retained a sense of identity. They had no land they could call their own, nor a universal bond of government. They have been exposed to diverse social influences, to the temptation of assimilation and the disintegrating force of extreme persecution—but they have not become extinct.

This extraordinary survival was foretold in Scripture: "Thus saith the Lord, who gives the sun for light by night, who stirs up the sea so that its waves roar—the Lord of Hosts is his name. If this fixed order departs

[8]A Study of History, Arnold Toynbee, Oxford University Press, 1957, Vol. I, page 194.

[9]Story of Civilization, Will Durant, Simon and Shuster

from me, says the Lord, then shall the descendants of Israel cease from being a nation before me forever." (Jer. 31:35-36)

To quote Pascal: "This people is not eminent solely by their antiquity, but is also singular by their duration, which has always continued from their origin till now. For whereas the nations of Greece and of Italy, of Lacedaemon, of Athens, and of Rome, and others who come long after, have long since perished, these ever remain, and in spite of the endeavors of many powerful kings who have a hundred times tried to destroy them, as their historians testify, and as it is easy to conjecture from the natural order of things during so long a space of years, they have nevertheless been preserved (and this preservation has been foretold); and extending from the earliest times to the latest, their history comprehends in its duration all our histories (which it preceded by a long time)."[10]

The biblical prophecy of Israel's scattering in case of disobedience is remarkable because such a scattering is not necessarily the result of foreign domination. The Romans, to whom the last and most extensive dispersion of the Jews was due, conquered many peoples who were generally allowed to remain in their land on the condition of submission to the Roman government. Because of the fanatic resistance and endless struggle of the Jews, the Romans became weary of slaughter and sold the people as slaves. They brought little money because the market was glutted with Jewish slaves and purchasers were hard to find. The number of slaves sold was beyond calculation. Since the destruction of Jerusalem the Jews have been scattered throughout the

[10]op. cit., page 174

world. But they retained their identity, a living fulfillment of the severe warning uttered by Moses: "If you will not obey the voice of the Lord your God, then all these curses shall come upon you and overtake you. You will be defeated before your enemies. You will be smitten with madness and blindness and confusion of mind. You shall grope at noonday as the blind grope in darkness and you shall not prosper in your ways. You shall be only oppressed and robbed continually and there shall be none to help you.

"The Lord will bring a nation against you from afar, from the end of the earth, as swift as the eagle flies, a nation whose language you do not understand. The Lord will scatter you among all peoples, from one end of the earth to the other; and there you shall serve other gods, of wood and stone, which neither you nor your fathers have known. And among these nations you will find no ease, and there shall be no rest for the sole of your foot; but the Lord will give you there a trembling heart, and failing eyes, and a languishing soul; your life shall hang in doubt before you; night and day you shall be in dread and have no assurance of your life.

"In the morning you shall say, 'Would it were evening!' And at evening you shall say, 'Would it were morning!' because of the dread which your heart shall feel and the sights which your eyes shall see." (Deut. 28) Moses adds: "You shall become a horror, a proverb, and a byword among all the peoples where the Lord will lead you away."

Some of the salient facts deserve further consideration:

► The announcement of a worldwide dispersion among nations where Israel shall find no ease,

► The concept of antisemitism,
► The fact that in spite of persecution the nation will survive and ultimately be led back to their homeland.

Scene 2

Post-biblical Times

The first item leads us to a brief review of Jewish history to illustrate the certainty of the prophetic word and the absolute sovereignty of God.

The greatest calamity that befell the Jewish nation was undoubtedly the destruction of Jerusalem and the temple in A.D. 70. Two years before, the Gentiles of Caesarea slew 20,000 Jews and sold thousands into slavery. In a single day the inhabitants of Damascus cut the throats of 10,000 Jews. During the actual siege of Jerusalem 116,000 bodies were thrown over the wall. After the fall of Jerusalem almost 100,000 fugitives were caught and sold as slaves. Many died as gladiators in the triumphal games. Josephus estimated that over one million people were killed in the siege and its aftermath.

A few years later, at about A.D. 115, the Jews of Cyrene, Egypt, Cyprus and Mesopotamia rose up against Rome. These uprisings were suppressed. Under Emperor Hadrian the Romans destroyed 985 towns in Palestine and slew 580,000 men. More perished through starvation, disease and fire. So many Jews were sold as slaves that their price fell to that of a horse. After that

Jews were not allowed in Jerusalem, except on one fixed day each year when they might come and weep before the ruins of the temple at the Wailing Wall.

One might have expected that the Jews would fare better after the nominal conversion of the Roman Empire to Christianity, but for both political and religious reasons this was not the case. The intention of discrimination was to prevent the inroads of Judaism by keeping its adherents from positions of authority. From discrimination to oppression was a short step.

The legal code of Theodosius (Roman emperor of the Eastern Roman Empire from A.D. 379-395) contained ideas of Jewish inferiority which permeated the whole of western law. The Byzantine Emperor Justinian III (A.D. 537-565) was the first emperor to interfere with religious institutions. The Byzantine emperors continued for two centuries the oppressive policies of Justinian toward the Jews. Heraclius banished them from Jerusalem (A.D. 628) and endeavored to exterminate them. Leo the Isaurian gave them the choice between Christianity or banishment. (A.D. 723)

When the first Crusade was launched in A.D. 1096, to recapture the holy places of Palestine from the Ottoman Muslims, the Crusaders thought it desirable to kill the Jews in Europe before proceeding to fight the Turks. Godfrey of Bouillon proclaimed that he would avenge the blood of Jesus upon the Jews and exterminate them all.

The second Crusade, launched in A.D. 1146-47, threatened to exceed the carnage of the first. A long series of violent assaults began.

The accusation of Jewish ritual murder was raised for the first time in A.D. 1144. Persecution raged in Ger-

many and also in Great Britain, especially from 1257 to 1267 when the Jewish communities in London, Canterbury, Winchester and Cambridge were almost wiped out.

In 1290 Edward I ordered the remaining Jews to leave the country by November 1. The same situation prevailed in France. In 1236 the Crusaders invaded the Jewish settlement of Anjou and Poitou and offered Christian baptism. When they refused, the Crusaders trampled 3,000 to death under their horses' hoofs. Jews were banished from France by Louis IX in 1254, but re-admitted a few years later. Phillip the Fair imprisoned some, confiscated their goods, and expelled 100,000 from France in 1306.

During the scourge of the Black Death in 1348-49, the charge that Jews poisoned the wells was current. At that time, many Jews migrated to Poland and Russia. In Spain conditions worsened and 1492 brought an edict of expulsion. The edict was imitated in Portugal in 1496. At that time the whole of western Europe was closed to Jews except for a few areas in northern Italy and Germany.

Toward the middle of the 17th century, the first persecutions in Poland broke out. The Jewish people yearned for the coming of the Messiah. David Reubeni of Arabia, although he did not claim to be the Messiah, was hailed by many Mediterranean Jews as their deliverer.

Perhaps the most famous imposter was Sabbatai Sebi. In 1648 the Jews of Smyrna heard the announcement that he was the promised Redeemer. Word spread through Jewish communities throughout the Ottoman Empire and thousands of Jews prepared to move to Palestine. The immediate effect was to discredit all Jews i

37

the eyes of the Turkish sultan who could no longer count on their political loyalty.

This allowed Greeks and Armenians to take over strategic functions in Ottoman society formerly held by Jews and in the second half of the 17th century the bulk of the Jewish community is said to have consisted of "depressed traitors, distressed artisans, distrusted bankers and discarded dragomen."[11] Ultimately Sabbatai Sebi was imprisoned by the Turkish authorities and accepted conversion to the Muslim faith.

Emancipation began to dawn for European Jews with the French Revolution in 1789. Two years later the emancipation in France became a historic fact. Alarming massacres occurred in the Ukraine in 1818. Antisemitism did not abate. The Dreyfus Affair in France in 1895, the massacres of Kichineff in 1903, demonstrated that antisemitism was still virulent. All this was mild in comparison with the extermination of six million Jews during World War II. This review certainly underscores the mournful accomplishment of the prophetic threat regarding national disobedience.

Antisemitism is one of the strange phenomena of history. Sociological factors are undoubtedly involved. The note of antisemitism, frequently echoed in the Greco-Roman world, was even sounded by outstanding intellectuals.

Juvenal attributed to the Jews an unwavering hostility toward the entire outside world. The Greeks failed in their attempt to hellenize the Jews of Israel and Egypt. At that point antisemitic literature multiplied. The religious and cultural divergencies were accentuated by frequent political clashes.

[11]*The Rise of the West*, William McNeill, page 639.

At the time of the destruction of the temple (A.D. 70) it is estimated that there were about seven million Jews in the Roman empire, representing about seven percent of the population. Their number, dress, life, custom of circumcision, property, ambition, prosperity, exclusiveness, intelligence, aversion to the worship of images and observation of the Sabbath day all aroused antisemitism which ranged from relatively harmless jokes to murder in the street.

Vespasian, under whose reign Jerusalem was destroyed, also closed the temple which had been erected in Egypt. He also demanded a special taxation, the fiscus Judaicus, which laid a foundation for special treatment of the Jewish people in the world.

Since the Jews have survived in spite of their dramatic history, it is strictly due to the sovereign power and plan of God who had announced both the scattering of the Jews and their ultimate return to Israel. Election is no guarantee of immunity against disaster. When Israel broke the Covenant she was exposed to God's judgment. This does not nullify God's decree of election or the ultimate realization of his purpose. God's compassionate love will prevail because he is merciful and gracious, slow to anger, and abounding in steadfast love and faithfulness, keeping steadfast love for thousands, forgiving iniquity and transgression and sin. (Exodus 34:6) His judgments have a definite purpose and will never go beyond the established limitation that he has set.

"When they are in the land of their enemies," said God, "I will not spurn them, neither will I abhor them so as to destroy them utterly and break my Covenant with them; for I am the Lord their God." (Lev. 26:44)

If the national disasters of heathen nations are a witness of the powerlessness of their gods, the disasters of Israel, on the contrary, are a demonstration of the reality of their God and his retributive justice. For this very reason the Old Testament history is not characterized by a narrow patriotism that concels national evil and misfortune.

The parable of Isaiah is most eloquent: "Does a farmer always plow and never sow? Is he forever harrowing the soil and never planting it? He knows just what to do, for God has made him see and understand. He doesn't thresh all grains the same. A sledge is never used on dill, but it is beaten with a stick. A threshing wheel is never rolled on cummin but it is beaten softly with a flail. Bread grain is easily crushed, so he doesn't keep on pounding it." (Isaiah 28:23 ff.)

This parable illustrates divine providence and God's action in relation to his own people. God does not always plow and harrow. The ultimate purpose is not destruction but harvest. The divine method is adapted to the soil and the grain. He prepares the ground and sows the seed, collects the harvest and separates the grain from the chaff. A harvest is always in view.

The fact that nations are used by God to carry out his judgment does not diminish their own responsibility. Historians have given various reasons for the decline of the Roman Empire. No doubt there were many cooperating factors, but it should not be overlooked that their cruel and heartless dispersion of the Jewish nation could not escape the retribution of God.

As God had previously used the Assyrians to punish Israel, so he later used the Roman Empire to scatter the Jews throughout the world. The Assyrians did not escape judgment for their cruel behavior dictated by national pride. The same holds true for other nations who have persecuted the Jews. At one point Spain was a world power with immense wealth gained through the discovery of the New World. Jewish people were expelled from Spain in 1492 and Spain later sank to secondary rank from which it never recovered. The recent downfall of Germany needs no documentation. Because the avowed purpose of Nasser and the Arab nations was not only to gain a military victory, but to obliterate the nation, to erase Israel from the map, and to bring their national identity to an end, their military defeat could be foreseen.

There is an intimate connection between the judgments on the Chosen People and the judgments of their oppressors. The judgment of Israel in point of time precedes that of the nations of the world, and the deliverance of Israel is effected by the judgment of the heathen world. The divine judgments on Israel should be a warning to other nations that divine judgment will also fall upon their sinfulness. This judgment will eventually result in the establishment of a divine kingdom.

What Habakkuk proclaims of the Chaldeans has universal implication: "Has not the Lord decreed that godless nations' gains will turn to ashes in their hands? They work so hard, but all in vain." The prophet adds: "The time will come when all the earth is filled, as the waters fill the sea, with an awareness of the glory of the Lord."

It may not be out of place to consider what may have precipitated the extraordinary judgment on Israel which has lasted so long. If idol worship in Israel resulted in the Babylonian captivity lasting 70 years, what national rebellion led to a dispersion which has lasted so long and a sorrow that wounded so deeply? Those who do not recognize the central significance of Jesus Christ would be hard pressed for an answer.

ACT III

THE RETURN

Just as God had announced that in case of national disobedience Israel would be scattered, so he also gave the assurance that Israel would be preserved in spite of persecution, and ultimately return to the land in unbelief. If, in the light of the geographic hazards, the national survival of Israel was surprising, then the survival during almost 2,000 years of exile in the face of severe persecution is almost unbelievable.

God had announced that "in that day the Lord will extend his hand yet a second time to recover the remnant which is left of his people, from Assyria, from Egypt, from Pathros, from Ethiopia (Cush), from Elam, from Shinar, from Hamath, and from the coastlands of the sea . . . He will assemble the outcasts of Israel and gather the dispersed of Judah from the four corners of the earth." (Isaiah 11:11, 12)

Notice the expression "a second time." The first exile known as the Babylonian Exile lasted only 70 years. The second time Israel has been dispersed to the four corners of the earth, but God would gather them from the "farthest part of the earth, among them the blind and the lame, the woman with child and her who is in travail, together; a great company, they shall return here." (Jer. 31:8) After the Babylonian captivity only a small company of Jews returned to Israel—approximately 50,000. The second time would bring them back from the four corners of the earth, perhaps even China (Isaiah 49:12—"Sinim"=China?).

After the return from Babylonia the Jews lamented the fact that they were slaves in their own land. "The rich yield of the land goes to the kings whom thou hast set over us because of our sins; they have power also over our bodies and over our cattle at their pleasure, and we are in great distress." (Neh. 9:36, 37)

The announcement of God concerning the final restoration is different: "I will restore the fortunes of my people Israel, and they shall rebuild the ruined cities and inhabit them; they shall plant vineyards and drink their wine, and they shall make gardens and eat their fruit. I will plant them upon their land, and they shall never again be plucked up out of the land which I have given them." (Amos 9:14, 15) After the return from the Babylonian Exile the Jews were dispersed to the four corners of the world. The final regathering is said to lead to a permanent planting in the land: They will no longer be uprooted.

One might expect that the prophetic word would indicate that the Jews' repentance and turning toward God would precede their return to the land. This was indeed the view of some early Zionist writers. However, the Scripture clearly says that the Jewish people would return to the land in unbelief:

"For I will take you from the nations, and gather you

44

from all the countries, and bring you into your own land. I will sprinkle clean water on you, and you shall be clean from all your uncleanness and from all your idols I will cleanse you. A new heart I will give you, and a new spirit I will put within you; and I will take out of your flesh the heart of stone and give you a heart of flesh. And I will put my spirit within you, and cause you to walk in my statutes and be careful to observe my ordinances. You shall dwell in the land which I gave to your fathers; and you shall be my people, and I will be your God." (Ezek. 36:24 ff. c.f. chap. 37)

It is needless to multiply the biblical quotations which have already been vindicated by the events of history. The Jews' return to the land is not justified by their righteousness but is carried out because of God's faithfulness to his promise. "The nations that are left around about you shall know that I, the Lord, have rebuilt the ruined places, and replanted that which was desolate; I. the Lord, have spoken, and I will do it." (Ezek. 36:36) See also Isaiah 48:9-11. As Paul puts in succinctly, the gifts and the call of God are irrevocable.

The extraordinary preservation in the land and miraculous survival throughout centuries of dispersion and persecution, the return to the land in unbelief, the creation of the nation of Israel—these prophecies clearly announced in the Word of God have now become historic realities. Just as surely God will also keep the explicit promise made in Amos: "I will plant them upon their land, and they shall never again be plucked up out of the land which I have given them." (Amos 9:15)

In May 1944 the *Reader's Digest* published a report on Palestine produced by Fredrick C. Painton. He wrote: "The Zionist has a fanatical spiritual belief in a greater

Palestine for the Jews; but the Arab picks up the soil in his hand and says that it is his and no third power in the world can take it away from him without a fight." Painton's final word is that "the Palestine problem will die out by sheer lack of Jews who would give up their homeland and plant themselves again in the sterile hills of Judea."

Even in 1944 this was a shrewd observation from the human standpoint. By that time some people might have foreseen a national restoration since some significant events had transpired. Zionism was on the move. Zionism is in many ways the continuation of the Jews' deepfelt attachment and strong religious allegiance to Palestine, the Promised Land.

At times the interest in the return of the Jews to Palestine was kept alive more by Christians than by the Jews themselves. It was only toward the end of the 19th century that Zionism found broader echoes in the Jewish world. Moses Hess wrote a book which combined ethical socialism, fervent nationalism and religious conservatism. It is interesting that the author insisted a moral and spiritual regeneration must precede the return to Israel. This was contrary to the Word of God and, as a matter of fact, it did not take place in that sequence. In 1873 the first agricultural settlement was established in Palestine by a group of Russian Jews called Lovers of Zion. Political Zionism received a strong impetus from Theodore Herzl whose brilliant gift enabled him to make a significant contribution. He was profoundly distressed by the antisemitism of the Dreyfus Affair in France. Although he preferred assimilation of the Jews into their own surrounding cultures he felt that a return to Israel was the only guarantee of national survival. Herzl had no living ties with Jewish and Hebrew traditional values.

The first Zionist congress was convened in 1897. The actual growth of the Jewish settlements in Palestine was due to the practical Zionists who moved to Palestine in small numbers and established settlements. By 1914 there were about 90,000 Jews in Palestine. The political Zionists insisted that the granting of a charter was an essential prerequisite for colonization. The opportunity came with World War I and the famous Balfour Declaration.

This was a letter written by Arthur J. Balfour, British foreign secretary, to Lord Rothschild, on November 2, 1917, declaring that: "His Majesty's Government views with favor the establishment in Palestine of a national home for the Jewish people, and will use their best endeavors to facilitate the achievement of this object, it being clearly understood that nothing shall be done which may prejudice the civil and religious rights of existing non-Jewish communities in Palestine, or the rights and political status enjoyed by Jews in any other country."

This declaration is carefully worded and speaks only of the establishment "in" Palestine of "a" national home. This concept, endorsed by the Allied powers and confirmed at San Remo in 1920, became the instrument of British and international policy.

As a result, 300,000 Jews had settled in Palestine by the end of 1935. The Arabs bitterly resisted Zionism and several times rose in revolt, especially in the period from 1936 through 1939. To reduce the strife, the British finally issued the White Paper of May 17, 1939, limiting immigration.

World War II atrocities gave renewed impetus to

Zionism and also stirred the sympathy of the world for the people without a country. At the same time, Arab nationalists intensified their demands for Arab rights in the area. Britain turned the problem over to the United Nations and on November 29, 1947, the U.N. called for partition of the territory into a Jewish and Arab state, linked in an economic union. Jerusalem was to be an international enclave under U.N. control.

The plan was rejected by the Arabs, and six months of confusion followed. The British mandate over the territory terminated May 15, 1948, but the Jews proclaimed the establishment of a sovereign Jewish State the previous day. Battles flared between furious Arabs and the Israelites, and U.N. mediation brought an uneasy armistice. Israel was admitted to U.N. membership on May 11, 1949.

Unrest increased once again in 1952 and tension increased. In 1956 Israel, Britain and France invaded Egypt in the famous "100 hour war." The Israeli objective was to destroy the raiding bases, to open sea communications through the Gulf of Aqaba and to pressure Egypt into serious peace negotiations. Britain and France sought control of the Suez Canal, which Egypt had taken over, but United Nations' pressure forced an end to hostilities. This was the uneasy peace that lasted until 1967.

Ezekiel's vision of the "dry bones" is well known. In answer to the question: "Can these bones live?" the prophet says, "O Lord God, thou knowest." It is explicitly stated that these bones are representative of the house of Israel. They say: "Our bones are dried up, and our hope is lost; we are clean cut off." God announces that he will open their graves and bring them home into the land of Israel. This will be followed by a new spiritual relationship with God.

Then the prophet sees the realization step by step; there was a noise and a rattling and the bones came together; next the muscles and flesh formed over the bones and skin covered them; finally the bodies began breathing and lived.

The dry bones are an apt picture of the Jewish nation before they returned to their land. It is here indicated that there will be successive and distinct stages of development. There is a preliminary organization and gradual implementation over a span of time. It often seems that great historic events appear abruptly on the scene. As a matter of fact, the underlying causes are usually at work over a period of time. Again, the events of 1967 are significant in pointing toward the fulfillment and climax of human history.

Scene 1

Jerusalem

The destruction of Jerusalem was graphically foretold in Luke 21. Christ had remarked that the things admired by the disciples, the beautiful stone work of the temple, would be knocked down and one stone would not be left on top of another. In answer to the question of the disciples as to when this would take place, Christ said:

"But when you see Jerusalem surrounded by armies, then know that its desolation has come near. Then let those who are in Judea flee to the mountains, and let those who are inside the city depart, and let not those who are out in the country enter it; for these are days of vengeance, to fulfill all that is written.

"Alas, for those who are with child and for those who give suck in those days! For great distress shall be upon the earth and wrath upon this people; they will fall by the edge of the sword, and be led captive among all nations; and Jerusalem will be trodden down by the Gentiles, until the times of the Gentiles are fulfilled." (21:20-24).

Less than 40 years later, in A.D. 70, Jerusalem was conquered by the Romans. On the tenth of Ab, in the year 70, amid circumstances of unparalleled horror, Jerusalem fell. The temple was burned and the Jewish State was no more. According to Josephus (c. A.D. 37-95), the Romans sent thousands of prisoners to the Egyptian mines. Multitudes perished in the Roman arenas by the sword and wild beasts. Those who were under 17 years of age were sold into slavery. Josephus estimated the total number of captives at 97,000 and the number of those who perished during the siege at some 1,100,000. It could be that Josephus' estimates are exaggerated, but it is certain that the nation suffered terribly and that these were indeed "days of vengeance," days of great distress.

Jesus had predicted that they would "fall by the edge of the sword," literally by "the mouth of the sword." The sword is poetically represented as a biting animal with a mouth devouring and destroying.

After the conquest, Vespasian, the Roman Emperor, considered Palestine his private possession. He gave large sections to his friends and favorites and allowed 800 Roman veterans to establish themselves close to the ruins of the city of Jerusalem. Even after the conquest a garrison was left behind to complete the work of demolition. The Jews were sent into captivity and scattered among all nations.

Even after these defeats the Jews did not submit passively. They held out until one by one their fortresses were reduced. They continued their fruitless and heroic efforts in Egypt. Under the reign of Trajan (A.D. 98-117) the Jews of Cyrene revolted. They were subdued in a struggle so fierce that the city never recovered.

Emperor Hadrian (A.D. 117-138) intended to found a Roman colony on the site of Jerusalem. This roused the Jewish people to a final revolt. For three years the conflict raged as the Jews fought with the energy of despair. The end came in A.D. 135, when Jerusalem fell.

Micah had announced that Jerusalem would be plowed like a field and become a heap of rubble. This was literally fulfilled. Hadrian ran the plowshare over the hill of Zion. The foundations of the new city were laid north of Jerusalem under the name of Aelia Capitolina. The city was inhabited by pagans. Jewish people were excluded from Jerusalem under the threat of death.

Jerusalem was indeed trodden down. Jewish people who wished to live in Judea had to buy the land from the victors. The Jewish attempt to rebuild the temple and restore the nation had failed.

Under the reign of the Emperor Julian the Apostate in A.D. 362, another attempt was made to rebuild the temple, but fire burst from the ruins and so terrified the workmen that the undertaking was abandoned.

In 1799, Napoleon issued a proclamation to the Asiatic Jews to rally to his standard and to regain and rebuild the Holy City. Strangely enough, the Syrian campaign of Napoleon was a total failure and his project did not materialize.

Napoleon had hoped to conquer Syria, which at the time included the present areas of Israel, Jordan, Syria and Lebanon. The city of Jaffa fell after a one-day siege, and Napoleon's army reached the fortress of Acre, which supposedly was indefensible. It looked like an easy victory.

A historian wrote: "There was no reason to expect that it could withstand Bonaparte's army of 13,000, but

Djezzar Pasha was as obstinate as he was cruel. . . . Bonaparte ordered one assault after another, each murderous and futile. The trenches were filling up with rotting corpses, which could not be removed, and each new wave of assailants had to step over their decomposing brothers. Meanwhile, the plague continued to rage. On May 20, after a two-month siege, Bonaparte gave it up and began his retreat to Egypt."[12]

In spite of determined attempts to have it otherwise, from the days of Titus (A.D. 70) until our own, Jerusalem has been "trodden down" by the Gentiles and the temple has not been rebuilt. Pagans, Christians and Mohammedans have at one time or another held the city, but the Jewish people never. Romans, Saracens and Crusaders have trampled the Holy City under foot. Only recently the Jewish State has been created, and the "times of the Gentiles" are obviously much closer to the end. Certainly the words of Christ regarding the condition of Jerusalem have been strikingly fulfilled.

It may not be easy to determine the full meaning of this fascinating announcement. The words "trodden down" could refer to contemptuous ill treatment or to actual occupation—in either case under Gentile supremacy. But sharp distinction between these conditions may not be necessary.

The word "Jerusalem" may need a more precise analysis. Is Jesus' reference limited to the city of Jerusalem? Could it mean, for instance, that other cities such as Jericho might flourish while Jerusalem is in abject misery? Does "Jerusalem" represent the entire country of Israel? In fact, is not the city representative of the

[12]J. Christopher Herold, *The Age of Napoleon*, American Heritage Publication Co., 1963, p. 76-78.

nation as a whole? Are not Jerusalem and Zion often used to designate the entire nation? In other words, does the prediction mean that the Jewish people will be trodden down for a long period of history, treated with contempt and live under Gentile supremacy? The text seems to indicate that not only Jerusalem would be in ashes or under Gentile control but that at the same time the nation of Israel would be scattered across the world and suffer contempt. Another interpretation says that only the city of Jerusalem is specifically intended here, that its welfare is the key to the ending of the "times of the Gentiles."

Times of the Gentiles

This leads up to a more careful examination of the expression "times of the Gentiles." Once again the question could be raised if this expression refers to foreign political supremacy over Jerusalem and the nation of Israel, or if it refers to the time of grace granted by God to the nations of the world. Both views have been advanced by reliable exegetes.

According to the Wycliffe Bible Commentary: "The phrase implies that God has scheduled a day of opportunity for the Gentiles, which will close with Israel's future restoration to favor." Similarly, Farrar, who identifies the times, or more literally the seasons, i.e., the opportunities of the Gentiles, as the periods allotted for their full evangelization. In this connection he refers to Romans 11:25: "Blindness in part has happened to Israel, until the fulness of the Gentiles be come in."

The same view is maintained by Godet. He points out that Jesus had previously spoken of the "time of visitation" in reference to the time of spiritual opportunity for Jerusalem. (Luke 19:44) Jerusalem had rejected this opportunity and now the Gentiles have their time of opportunity.

It is suggested that the plural word might refer to the shifting times in which every nation has a time of visitation. In other words, the destruction of Jerusalem signaled the end of the times of opportunity for Israel as a nation and now the times of the Gentiles would begin for them to enter into the kingdom of God. Since the city would be in the power of the Gentiles during this time and since the words Jerusalem and Zion often stand for the people of the Lord under the Old Covenant, the expression also implies that the Jewish people would be oppressed during this period of time. It is pointed out by these expositors that any other interpretation of the text would have Jesus saying that the Gentiles will have supremacy over Jerusalem until they no longer have supremacy over Jerusalem.

In spite of these arguments, many Bible expositors maintain that the political supremacy of the Gentiles is in view here. This is maintained by H. A. W. Meyer, Lange, and others. It is remarkable that these two conditions have coincided so far, that this has been a time of spiritual opportunity for the Gentiles and at the same time the Jewish people have been oppressed politically. It is clear that the Jewish nation as a whole missed their great day of national opportunity. Although God has not rejected his people, they have stumbled spiritually and salvation has been proclaimed to the Gentiles. (Romans 11) This is indeed a great day of opportunity for the Gentile nations, the day of opportunity for the Church to proclaim the salvation of God to all nations. At the same time Jerusalem has been politically insignificant and the Jewish people have been "trodden down" in the various countries of their residence.

Still other Bible expositors have taught that the times of the Gentiles began with the captivity of Judah under Nebuchadnezzar because since that time Jerusalem has been under Gentile overlordship. [13] But from the immediate biblical context it would seem that the "times" begin with the destruction of Jerusalem in A.D. 70. It should be noted that the definite article "the" is not found in the original. There is no reference to THE well known times of the Gentiles. The context requires a time indication as to how long Israel shall be trodden down— not the starting time. It is precisely because the time of distress lasts until the return of the Lord that the next verses announce his return.

It is crucial to us that the times of the Gentiles will come to an end. According to Christ, the times of the Gentiles will last until the divine judgment on Jerusalem carried out by the Gentiles will have come to an end. The plural (times, literally seasons) seems to indicate that there are many constituent parts or segments in the historical development and fulfillment.

The end of those times coincides with the return of Christ. This is indicated in the immediate context: "And there will be signs in sun and moon and stars, and upon the earth distress of nations and perplexity at the roar of the sea and the waves, men fainting with fear and with foreboding of what is coming on the world; for the powers of the heavens will be shaken. And then they will see the Son of Man coming in a cloud with power and great glory. Now when these things begin to take

[13]Von Hofmann, in *Der Schriftbeweis*, Nördlingen, 1857, II. 2. 642 ff.

place, look up and raise your heads because your redemption is drawing near." (21:25-28)

This is somewhat reminiscent of Daniel 7. The prophet has a vision of four beasts symbolic of various world empires. Finally their dominion is taken away and someone like the Son of Man comes with the clouds of heaven. To him was given the dominion and glory and kingdom, so that all peoples, nations, and languages should serve him. His dominion is an everlasting dominion which shall not pass away.

In the same context the prophet indicates that the kingdom and the dominion and the greatness of the kingdoms under the whole heavens shall be given to the people of the saints of the Most High. (Dan. 7:27)

If the times of the Gentiles are immediately followed by the return of Jesus Christ, it is obvious that:

► the times of the Gentiles do not come to an end when Israel returns to the land and when Jerusalem is once more in Jewish hands,

► that it is most reasonable to assume that until Christ's return, Jerusalem, the country and the people will be in turmoil.

A related text should not be overlooked in this connection. Jesus said: "O Jerusalem, Jerusalem, killing the prophets and stoning those who are sent to you! How often would I have gathered your children together as a hen gathers her brood under her wings, and you would not! Behold, your house is forsaken and desolate. For I tell you, you will not see me again, until you say, 'Blessed be he who comes in the name of the Lord.'" (Matt. 23:37-39)

The Greek text is somewhat uncertain regarding the words "and desolate." The present tense indicates that this is a moment of tragic and decisive significance. The time for divine help and protection is past and the final result will be that they themselves must take care of the house, which will result in desolation and destruction.

The words "your house" might refer to the temple, or the city which Jesus had just addressed, or even the entire nation of which Jerusalem and the temple were representative. This period of desolation will continue until, as a nation, they will say: "Blessed be he who comes in the name of the Lord." He will be received with this Messianic greeting at the moment of national conversion when he shall appear in Messianic glory.

This moment of his return signals the end of the times of the Gentiles. H. A. W. Meyer writes: "Jesus is addressing Jerusalem, and threatening it with the withdrawal of God's superintending care, and that until the second appearance of the Messiah." [14] The manifestation of his glory will sweep away all doubt and opposition and Israel will at last acknowledge and confess Christ to be their deliverer.

There certainly is a tragic note in these words with which Jesus bids farewell to Jerusalem. Although the immediate prospect is dark, there is also the certainty of ultimate spiritual victory. The desolation of the house which is announced here is a concept very similar to the one expressed by Luke when he speaks of the downtrodden situation of Israel. From this moment on the house is abandoned to their own care. Those who could and would have saved Israel gave up further effort. The Messiah will no longer trouble them until their mood changes, until they are ready to receive him with the ancient Messianic salutation. At the triumphal entry

[14]H. A. W. Meyer, in loco.

58

into Jerusalem some had indeed greeted him in this fashion, but the people in general refused to acknowledge him. It is only at his triumphal return that the nation as a whole will recognize him as the promised Messiah who comes in the name of the Lord.

God often used other nations to chastise Israel. Centuries ago Isaiah viewed the Assyrian invasion in this way. The prophet described Assyria as a whip of divine anger used against the godless nation. Assyria, however, was not conscious of the divine plan and only intent on destruction and world conquest. The pride and arrogance of Assyria will also be judged. (Isaiah 10:5-11)

When the Lord has finished his strange work of judgment against Zion, he will punish the arrogant boasting of the king of Assyria and his haughty pride. "Shall the ax boast greater power than the man who uses it? Is the saw greater than the man who saws? Can a rod strike until the hand is moving it? Can a cane walk by itself?" (10:15) Assyria stands as an ax, a saw, a rod, a cane in the providence of God.

History repeats itself on a vast scale. God uses the nations to punish Israel. The times of Gentile supremacy has lasted for centuries. They are to be followed by the return of Jesus Christ and, as of old, he will judge those who have destroyed Israel.

The abrupt change in the prophetic discourse of Christ is most remarkable. He speaks of the times of the Gentiles and in the next verse of the distress of nations in perplexity. This sudden change is due to the return of Jesus Christ. Christ moves from the judgment of Jerusalem to the judgment of the earth because every judgment in the course of history prefigures the final one.

The nations who had triumphed over Israel are now seen as distressed, perplexed, fainting and under judgment. The Lord uses the nations to deal with Israel, but as Assyria of old, he now submits them to his sovereign judgment.

Other Scriptures confirm that Jerusalem will suffer great calamity and that the "downtroddenness" will reach a climax toward the end time. "Alas, in all history, when has there ever been a time of terror such as in the coming day? It is a time of trouble for my people—for Jacob—such as they have never known before. Yet God will rescue them! For on that day, says the Lord of Hosts, I will break the yoke from their necks and snap their chains, and foreigners shall no longer be their masters!" (Jer. 30:7,8)

The emphasis falls again on the fact that the ultimate deliverance will come from God and is not due to a military victory of Israel. In fact, according to Zechariah, the Lord will gather together the nations to fight Jerusalem. The city will be taken, the houses rifled, the loot divided and the women raped. Half the population will be taken away as slaves and half will be left in what remains of the city. Then the Lord will go out fully armed for war, to fight against those nations. That day his feet will stand upon the Mount of Olives to the east of Jerusalem. (Zech. 14:1-4)

God is presented as a Mighty Conqueror whose return will deliver the nation in extreme peril. At that point, Jerusalem and Judah will be like a cup of poison to all the nearby nations that sent their armies to surround Jerusalem. The city will be a heavy stone burdening the world. Though all the nations of the earth unite in an attempt to move her, they will all be crushed. "In that day," says the Lord, "I will bewilder the armies drawn up against her and make fools of them. I will watch over the people of Judah, but blind all her enemies." No wonder that the time of Gentile supremacy is succeeded by one of fear and trembling and foreboding of what is coming on the world.

To sum up, Jesus definitely announced the destruction of Jerusalem which took place in A.D. 70. He predicted periods of Gentile supremacy and of spiritual opportunity. He announced that this period will come to an end with his own return. The word Jerusalem seems to stand not only for the city, but for the land as a whole and, perhaps, for the situation of the Jewish people as a whole. As to the city itself, it is not certain that Israel will remain in possession of Jerusalem. As to the land, the ancient boundaries do not coincide with the modern area of Israel, and in this sense "Jerusalem" is still "downtrodden." As far as the nation as a whole is concerned, it is also true that to this day many are "downtrodden" in various countries of the world, especially in Russia.

Contemporary events are significant in discovering the first steps toward the end of Gentile supremacy. The foundation of the Jewish State has been established and many reverses could take place before Gentile supremacy comes to an end. In fact, according to the prophetic word, it is to be expected that Jerusalem will ultimately be surrounded and practically conquered before deliverance will come.

The extraordinary victory of the Israeli army in 1967 should not be misleading. It was indeed an astonishing military victory. The battle was swift and the victory decisive, but the real issue is elsewhere. Although most of the nations of the world have accepted and acknowledged the right of Israel to exist, this is not the case for the Arabs. Even after their disastrous defeat the Arab leaders still proclaimed that their ambition is to build up sufficient strength to eradicate the State of Israel. It will not be easy for the Arab nations to forget their crushing defeat and it is not difficult to foresee further wars.

God has guaranteed the existence of Israel; he has predicted the return of the Jews to Palestine, and, therefore, it will not be possible to eradicate the State of Israel. A military victory on the part of the Arabs would have been conceivable—in fact, might have been expected. But as long as the purpose of the Arab leaders is to wipe out Israel as a nation their efforts will be frustrated because they are contrary to the prophetic word of God. At the same time, Scripture tells that Jerusalem will suffer extreme distress and will ultimately be delivered only through the direct intervention of Jesus Christ. It is in this light that the present developments are significant because they are the type of event which one might expect as history moves toward a climax. It is, of course, impossible to foresee how long these conflicts will last and when the cataclysmic denouement will take place.

The Temple

In one of his letters the apostle Paul speaks of the son of perdition, the Antichrist "who opposes and exalts himself against every so-called god or object of worship, so that he takes his seat in the temple of God, proclaiming himself to be God." (II Thess. 2:4)

Some of the early church fathers expected a literal fulfillment. Irenaeus (A.D. 120-202) wrote: "When this Antichrist shall have devastated all things in the world, he will reign for three years and six months and sit in the temple of Jerusalem." (*Against Heresies*, Book V, chap. 30, par. 4) Since by that time the temple of Jerusalem had already been destroyed, Irenaeus must have expected the reconstruction of the temple.

Chrysostom (A.D. 347-407), writing a little later, takes a different view. He explains that the Antichrist "will be seated in the temple of God, not that in Jerusalem only but also in every church." (in loco)

Paul sometimes uses the word temple figuratively to describe the Church of Christ: Ephesians 2:21; I Corinthians 6:19; II Corinthians 6:16. The exact meaning of the text would have to be determined by the context. Several considerations add weight to the literal viewpoint:

► He *sits*, or takes his seat in the temple of God;

► The usage of the definite article, *the* temple of God;

► The definite relationship and dependence of the entire passage on Daniel 11:36;

► The possible relationship with Matthew 25:15 and Mark 13:14; in this last passage the masculine participle may indicate a person rather than an image;

► The possible relationship with Daniel 12:11.

For these reasons the literal interpretation is maintained by DeWette, Lünemann, Wieseler, Döllinger and Milligan, to mention a few.

Augustine took an intermediate position: "It is uncertain in what temple he will sit, whether in that ruin of the temple which was built by Solomon, or in the Church. For the apostle would not call the temple of any idol or demon the temple of God. And on this account some think that in this passage Antichrist means not himself alone, but his whole body, that is, the mass of men who adhere to him, along with him their prince; and they also think that we should render the Greek more exactly were we to read, not 'in the temple of God,' but 'for' or 'as the temple of God,' as if he himself were the temple of God, the Church."[15]

The argument of Augustine that Paul would not call the temple of any idol or demon the temple of God is used by H. A. W. Meyer to accentuate Irenaeus' position: "On account of the definite expression 'sit' it cannot be otherwise understood than in its *proper* sense. But on account of the repetition of the article can only *one definite temple* of *one definite true God*—that is, the temple of Jerusalem—be meant." (in loco)

If this is to be understood literally, and much in the text and context seems to favor it, then it would demand that the Jewish people rebuild the temple. This is conceivable because:

▶ There is sufficient religious sentiment in the nation;

▶ It would be a good political move to create a symbol of cultural and religious unity for all Jews, religious and non-religious, both in Israel and for those who are still in the diaspora.

A problem would arise inasmuch as those motivated by religious feeling would want the temple erected on the ancient and hallowed site presently occupied by the Dome of the Rock. That this would lead to very serious complications is beyond doubt. How the sacred mosque of Muslims would be demolished, if by an act of God (earthquake) or by deliberate plan, cannot be

[15]*The City of God*, Book XX, chap. 19, par. 1. Augustine.

foreseen. The issue might be compromised by erection elsewhere of the future temple.

It must not be overlooked that many Orthodox Jews feel that the secular State of Israel cannot possibly embody the religious aspiration of the Jews. According to Rabbi Elmer Berger, executive vice president of the antizionist American Council for Judaism, Israel's territorial claims to the old city of Jerusalem have no foundation in Judaism.

He declares that the military victories of Israel in 1967 cannot be seen as a fulfillment of the spiritual aspiration of many Jews with respect to the Zion of the religious faith.[16] The tension between those motivated by political, sociological and nationalistic views and those motivated by religious aspiration will increase in the future, and have already been very troublesome in the land of Israel. It may be pointless to pursue speculations, but at any rate it is not difficult to foresee a literal fulfillmcnt should this be the intent of Scripture.

[16]*Chicago Tribune,* June 22, 1967.

Scene 2

Surrounding Nations

Egypt

The history of Israel cannot be understood without frequent reference to the history of Egypt. It is perhaps symbolic that the very earliest recorded mention of Israel outside of the Scriptures occurs on a victory stele or stone pillar erected by the Egyptian King Marniptah about 1220 B.C. At that time Israel had barely conquered part of Canaan. Western Palestine had been subject to Egyptian rule for many centuries, and the Israeli conquest of Canaan led to collision with Egypt. The ancient stele informs us: "The people of Israel is desolate; it has no offspring."

The first reference to Israel as a nation in the Scriptures is found in Exodus 6:6, describing the situation of the Jews *in Egypt* before the Exodus. The Exodus itself produced tension between Egypt and Israel. According to the famous Orientalist W. F. Albright, "Evidence for the substantial historicity of the account of the Exodus and the wandering in the regions of Sinai, Midian, and Kadesh, can easily be given, thanks to our greatly increased knowledge of topography and archaeology."[17]

For the next thousand years of Israeli history Egypt is always seen in the background, occasionally casting a long shadow over Israel, threatening, conquering, controlling. Most significant, perhaps, was the invasion of Shishak shortly after the death of Solomon. A huge Egyptian host carried fire and sword over the country, devastating many cities. In the great Karnak list, Shishak listed over 150 places which he claimed to have taken.

At other times Egypt became an unreliable ally. This foreign entanglement was often denounced by the prophets, as in Ezekiel's rueful analogy, "As Israel leaned on your back, like a cracked staff, you snapped beneath her hand and wrenched her shoulder out of joint and made her stagger with the pain." (Ezekiel 29:7)

That Egypt occupies a significant place in the Scriptures is not surprising. Egypt was one of the first advanced societies and this was largely due to two factors: the grain-centered agriculture of the Middle East provided an adequate basis for civilization; the River Nile allowed irrigation that was vital to early civilizations and regular production of food supplies. At the same time irrigation demanded a coordinated effort, organization and supervision.

It is not surprising that early civilizations are centered around major rivers: the Nile for Egypt, the Euphrates for Mesopotamia, the Ganges for India and the Yangtse for China.

[17]*From the Stone Age to Christianity*, W. F. Albright, Doubleday & Co., New York, 1957, page 255.

Egypt was one of the great world powers. Egyptian dynasties succeeded each other with varying degrees of glory and decline, reaching their heyday of power under the New Empire (1570-1150 B.C.). It was during that time that the Exodus took place; God had revealed himself as the one who brought Israel out of the land of Egypt, out of the house of bondage.

Egypt was not beyond the prophetic vision of the ancient seers. Jeremiah proclaimed that not only the kingdom of Judah, but all the surrounding nations would come under the control of the king of Babylon: "And now the Lord says this to the evil nations, the nations surrounding the land that God gave his people Israel: See, I will force you from your land just as Judah will be forced from hers; but afterwards I will return and have compassion on all of you, and will bring you home to your own land again, each man to his inheritance. . . . Israel and her neighboring lands shall serve the king of Babylon for 70 years." (12:12,14; 25:11) This announcement was fulfilled with striking accuracy.

Similarly, Ezekiel announced the downfall of Egypt: "For you have said, 'The Nile is mine; I have made it for myself!' . . . Therefore the Lord God said: 'I will bring an army against you, O Egypt, and destroy both men and herds. The land of Egypt shall become a desolate wasteland. . . . I will utterly destroy the land of Egypt, from Migdol to Syene, as far south as the border of Ethiopia.' " (chap. 29)

At the same time he announces that Egypt will be restored and that the Egyptians will return from banishment. But the prophet adds that afterward Egypt "will be an unimportant minor kingdom." (29:14) "It shall be the most lowly of the kingdoms, and never again exalt itself above the nations; and I will make them so small that they will never again rule over the nations."

"Historically this has been eminently true," comments F. Gardiner. "For a little while Egypt struggled against its oppressors, but its power was already broken, and from the time of its conquest by Cambyses it has never been for any length of time independent. There are few stronger contrasts in any inhabited country than between the ancient glory, dignity, power and wealth of Egypt, and its later insignificance."[18]

The prophetic announcement regarding the minor role of Egypt is indeed extraordinary. There was absolutely no human reason to anticipate such a turn of events. The power of Babylonia did not last much longer than the life of Nebuchadnezzar. One might have expected that Egypt, along with other nations, would once again enjoy freedom and power and rise to a place of preeminence.

For one brief moment it did seem that the old Egyptian glory would return, but the power vacuum created by the decline of Babylonia did not last. Persia emerged as a major power and the energetic Cambyses invaded Egypt in 525 B.C. In vain did Amasis, king of Egypt, endeavor to rescue the empire through an alliance with Greek mercenaries. His son, Psamtik III, could not stop the invaders and fell before the invading forces of Cyrus of Persia. Soon all of Egypt was occupied and became a Persian province.

The Persians controlled Egypt until they were succeeded by the Greeks under the leadership of Alexander the Great (332 B.C.)

[18]*The Bible Commentary for Bible Students*, F. Gardiner, edited by Charles John Elicott, Marshall Brothers, London, in loco.

In turn, the Romans dispossessed the Greeks and became the new masters of Egypt. The Roman period lasted until the Muslim conquest. It took only a small army of 4,000 men followed by a second expeditionary corps of 12,000 men to subdue Egypt and defeat the Romans in A.D. 640. For the next 300 years Egypt was simply a province of the Eastern Caliphate.

The early caliphs were immediate successors of Mohammed and ruled Egypt from Medina in Arabia. A little later the capital was transferred north to Damascus and around A.D. 750 to Baghdad. Dynasties followed each other with various degrees of independence, among them the famous Mamelukes. True independence was never regained as Egypt stood always in relationship to the Caliphate.

In 1517 Egypt became part of the Ottoman Empire, governed from Constantinople. Napoleon's Syrian campaign led to French occupation of Egypt, and British occupation brings us to modern times. It was in 1914 that Egypt became a British protectorate, and only in recent years was independence gradually obtained.

This quick review bears out the remarkable prediction of Ezekiel, that although Egypt would be restored and not be annihilated as some of the other nations which disappeared in the night of history, the nation would never again be a significant world power. To this very day the word of Ezekiel is being fulfilled. Egypt shall not become a world power regardless of the giant dreams of Egyptian nationalists.

This does not mean that Egypt could not defeat Israel nor lead an Arab coalition. But the position once occupied by Egypt was similar to the one now enjoyed by the "Big Two" of the atomic era, and that has been lost irrevocably. No one could have guessed such an abrupt and permanent change, but the prophets foretold it under divine inspiration.

Interestingly, the biblical indications regarding Egypt do not stop at this point. It is the view of most ancient and modern interpreters that the events referred to by Daniel in chapter 11:36 ff. refer to the future, to the time of the Antichrist.* This is undoubtedly the best interpretation of the text. This view is justified because:
► Daniel 11:36 is echoed by Paul in II Thessalonians 2:4 where he refers distinctly to the Antichrist;
► Verse 40 speaks specifically of the time of the end and the entire section (vv. 40-45) is immediately followed by an announcement of a final time of trouble and the resurrection (12:1,2).

It is stated in this passage that, "At the time of the end the king of the south shall attack the king previously described, the one who shall exalt himself and magnify himself above every god," i.e., the Antichrist.

The king of the south is not difficult to identify because throughout the entire chapter he is identified with Egypt. (11:8) Our text is no exception. The prophet adds that this attack will backfire because the Antichrist will invade various lands including Israel and overthrow the governments of many nations. "He shall stretch out his hand against the countries, and the land of Egypt shall not escape. He shall become ruler of the treasures of gold and of silver, and all the precious things of Egypt." (11:41,42)

This prophetic view of the end time presupposes that:
► Egypt will continue to exist throughout history;

*This was the view of Jerome, Luther, Keil, Klieforth, to name a few. Speaking of verses 40-45, the *Interpreter's Bible* states: "This section contains a prediction of events leading up to the end."

► As predicted by Ezekiel, Egypt will no longer be a major world power;

► Egypt will be of sufficient strength to risk an attack—this would imply a measure of independence, which is now an accomplished fact;

► There will be a relative amount of wealth in Egypt in the end times.

Even this is not the last word of prophecy regarding Egypt. Because of the long standing enmity between Egypt and Israel one might expect an announcement of ultimate doom. Actually this is not the case. The prophetic word announces that "the Lord will make himself known to the Egyptians. They will know the Lord. The Egyptians will turn to the Lord and he will listen to their plea and heal them. In that day Israel will be an ally of Egypt and ultimately God will say: 'Blessed be Egypt, my people.' " (Isaiah 19:21-25)

A detailed analysis of Isaiah 19 is beyond the limits of this book, but the ultimate conclusion is crystal clear: the bitter enmity has come to an end and Israel and Egypt are now reconciled to God and, therefore, to each other. Nothing could better demonstrate the universal purposes of the God of grace.

By way of contrast it is interesting that Jeremiah announced that the city of Babylon would be destroyed and that it would be abandoned forever. Babylon shall sink, nevermore to rise. (Jer. 51:61-64) Similarly, Isaiah states that Babylon, the most glorious of kingdoms and flower of Chaldean culture, will be as utterly destroyed as Sodom and Gomorrah. Babylon will never rise again. Generation after generation will come and go, but the land will never again be lived in. The wild animals of the desert will make it their home. Ostriches will live there, hyenas and jackals will den within the palaces. (Isaiah 13)

This was not to be expected because Babylon was one of the major cities of the ancient world. But only ruins remain from the glorious city built by Nebuchadnezzar and his father. The city was captured by the Persians and later taken over by the Greeks. By 275 B.C. the inhabitants were removed to a new city. With that event the history of Babylon ends. To this day the topography of ancient Babylon is far from clear.

Jerusalem shall be trodden down . . . Egypt will continue as a nation but in a weakened position . . . Babylon will be uninhabited and never rise from its fall . . . these are predictions which have been verified in the course of history without a shadow of a doubt.

Sudan

Occasionally the Scripture speaks of the land of Cush. Sometimes the Hebrew word has simply been transliterated and so the Authorized Version speaks of the land of Cush in Isaiah 11:11, where the Revised Standard Version has "Ethiopia." At other times the word Cush is translated Ethiopia in the A.V., as in Genesis 2:13, where the R.S.V. reads Cush.

The exact geographic location or identification of Cush has been a matter of dispute. It is generally recognized that Genesis 2:13 refers to a Cush located in Asia. Most of the other places, however, where Cush is found in association with Egypt, refer to the African Cush. A glance at the map will indicate that a connection between the two would not be difficult if the Cushites lived south of Egypt, close to the Red Sea, and also on the other side of the Red Sea in the Arabian peninsula.

Wherever the Cushites are associated with Egypt, the reference is to an area immediately south of Egypt and west of the Red Sea.

In ancient times this area was called Ethiopia, but since modern Ethiopia is the same as Abyssinia this is confusing. The ancient Cush is really the equivalent of the modern Sudan. At Kerma, notes the historian, "The archaeologist Reisner excavated an Egyptian fortress dating from the 11th and 12th dynasties, with inscriptions from which it appears that this represented the colonial garrison of an indigenous Sudanese principality called Cush, lying between the third and fourth cataracts of the Nile."[19]

Cush was an Egyptianized kingdom which emerged toward 1000 B.C. and survived until about A.D. 350. Around 600 B.C. the Cushites enlarged their borders to the south, moving their capital to Meroe. The new frontier was probably a little to the south of Khartoum. "All this was the land of the blacks, and the Cushite dynasty henceforward ruled over a mixed population of Caucasians and Negroes, with the Negroes no doubt predominating." [20]

Up to that point Cush, like Egypt, had been basically a country of white Caucasians. It is therefore interesting to note that precisely at that time Jeremiah raised the question: "Can the Ethiopian (Cushite) change his skin, or the leopard his spots?" (13:23)

Ezekiel had announced that the land of Cush would also fall into the hands of Nebuchadnezzar. (30:1-10)

[19]*A Short History of Africa*, Rowland Oliver and J. D. Fage, Penguin Books, Baltimore, Maryland, 1965, page 39.
[20]Ibid. page 40.

More interesting is the fact that the very same passage in the prophecy of Daniel which speaks of a battle between Egypt and the Antichrist indicates that the latter will not only conquer Egypt, but that "the Ethiopians (Cushites) shall be at his steps," (Daniel 11:43) i.e., they shall follow in his train or be his servants. Because of their alliance with Egypt, the Cushites—modern Sudan—will also be overrun.

Once again it is remarkable that the final word of God regarding the Cushites is positive. They will stretch out their hands to God in adoration and ultimately recognize that the God of Scripture is the true God. (Psalm 68:31, Isaiah 45:14; c.f. Psalm 87:4) It is true that in the Scriptures the Cushites are viewed as representatives of the remotest nations. At the same time there is no reason not to look forward to the actual fulfillment of these glorious words concerning both Egypt and the Sudan.

Libya

Along with the Egyptians and Cushites the Libyans are also mentioned in the prophetic text of Daniel 11:43. The Hebrew word Lubim describes the Libyans in the narrower sense. Another Hebrew word, Put, designates the Libyans in the broader sense, those who had spread out over the northern part of Africa as far as Mauritania. Put is mentioned several times in the Old Testament as a warlike people furnishing auxiliaries to Egypt and generally associated with both Libya and the Cushites.

Perhaps the Lubim refers more directly to the Libyans immediately adjacent to Egypt. It was only in 1949 that the United Nations decided that an independent state of Libya should be formed no later than January 1, 1952. Modern Libya roughly corresponds to the ancient area of Lubim and, therefore, the translation "Libya" is quite justified. Libya was admitted to the Arab League on July 29, 1953.

It is of interest that at the time of the end Egypt will be in alliance with Libya and the Sudan. The ancient and traditional alliance of Egypt, Cush (Sudan), the Lubim or Libya, and Put (covering North Africa almost from Egypt to Mauritania) will exist once more. The present alignment of power is not accidental. The national independence of these nations and their common perspective certainly foreshadows the situation we can expect in the end according to the prophet Daniel.* Cush and Put (the broader concept of Libya embracing most of North Africa) are also mentioned together in Ezekiel 38:5; Egypt is not mentioned in the context.

Ammon And Moab

The Ammonites were closely related to the Moabites, almost to the point of identity. In biblical writings one is occasionally spoken of under the name of the other. The precise position of their respective territories is difficult to determine. The one major city of the Ammonites was the fortress of Rabbah, northeast of the Dead Sea. The modern city of Amman—since 1950 the capital of Jordan—is the ancient Rabbah-Ammon. Whereas the

---

*It is interesting that in Ezekiel 38 Israel's ancient foes such as Ammon, Moab, Edom, along with the old imperial powers such as Egypt and Babel are not enumerated. Among the peoples that are mentioned are those living at the extreme north (verse 6) and east (Persia in verse 5) and south (Ethiopia or Cush in verse 5), representing the borders of the then-known world. The fact that occasionally Cush and Put are symbolically representative of remote nations does not preclude the possibility of literal fulfillment, especially when Egypt is found in the same context in Daniel 11.

Ammonites formed the Bedouin section, the Moabites were a more settled nation. Neither one ever obtained a solid footing on the west side of the Jordan.

The relationship between these tribes and Israel was stormy from the start. The Ammonites and Moabites were excluded from the national life of Israel. (Deut. 23:4) Occasional excursions on their part into Israel were generally repulsed.

We know very little about the Ammonites and Moabites outside of biblical sources. Shalmaneser III mentions a small contingent of a thousand Ammonite men in the allied army which fought against him at Karkar in 853 B.C. About a century later Tiglath-Pileser III received tribute from Ammon. Jeremiah predicted that they would be destroyed by Nebuchadnezzar. (49:1-6) According to Josephus, this was fulfilled five years after the fall of Jerusalem.

It would seem, however, that they submitted to Nebuchadnezzar and at one point Ammonite troops were among those who sacked Jerusalem. Toward that time some of the Jewish people took refuge among the Ammonites (Jer. 40:11) but hostility flared up again. After this Jewish debacle the Ammonites took possession of some of the cities of Gad from which the Jewish population had been removed by the king of Babylon. (Jer. 49:1-6) In spite of all this, Jeremiah does predict that the fortunes of the Ammonites will be restored.

General hostility continued even after the Babylonian Exile. The Ammonites opposed the restoration led by Nehemiah. In his book they are found in coalition with the Arabians. (4:7) The same coalition opposed Judas Maccabee. The apocryphal Book of the Maccabees describes them as a mighty and numerous people, and Justin Martyr (c. A.D. 100-165) still mentions them as being rather numerous, but Origen (c. A.D. 185-254) includes the country under the general name of Arabia. The area was indeed gradually occupied by the Arabian Nabataens.

In Daniel 11:41—a passage which definitely refers to the Antichrist—it is stated that he will come into the glorious land, i.e., Israel, but that some shall be delivered out of his hand, namely the main part of the Ammonites, along with Edom and Moab. It may be that these nations are merely mentioned as typical enemies of Israel, symbolic of future enemies, or that this is a reference to distinct national entities.

In this connection Isaiah predicts that when God gathers the dispersed of Judah from the four corners of the earth, those who harass Judah shall be cut off and Israel shall put forth her hand against Edom and Moab, and the Ammonites shall obey them. (Isaiah 11:11-14)

It may not be easy from the context to determine the moment of this triumph or its nature, but the distinct reference to these nations might be significant. It is true that they could be representative of the ancient enemies in the immediate vicinity of Israel. But from a practical standpoint this would make little difference. In the context of Daniel 11 the reference to Egypt is certainly to be taken literally, and so it may be best to assume that the other references are also to be understood literally. The fact that Ammon, Edom and Moab would be spared by the power of the Antichrist—at least the main part of the Ammonites—might possibly indicate that they would be in agreement with him. This is a matter for speculation.

The Ammonites always lived to the north and northeast of Moab. Today both territories are part of Jordan. Although we have a little more information regarding the history of Moab, our sources are rather meager. Moab is also mentioned in Daniel 11 and Isaiah 11, and Jeremiah says distinctly that in the latter days the fortunes of Moab will be restored. (48:47) Essentially the histories of Ammon and Moab run parallel. Whether the reference is symbolic or literal, they are mentioned together both in relation to the Antichrist and in relation to the triumph of Israel. (Daniel 11:41; Isaiah 11:14)

Edom

Edom occupied the area of Mount Seir, a territory east of the Dead Sea, and the Arabah, the great valley extending between the south end of the Dead Sea and the Gulf of Aqaba. When the migrating Israelites came to the border of Edom, passage through Edomite territory was refused. Although Israel was admonished, "You shall not abhor an Edomite, for he is your brother," (Deut. 23:7) Edom and Judah were engaged in war with each other throughout most of their history.

The primary contention was to determine control of the Arabah rift stretching between them. This was of great importance because of the trade route which followed its length and because of its copper and iron deposits. The Promised Land had been described as one whose stones were iron and out of whose hills you can dig copper. (Deut. 8:9)

Although no reference is found in Scripture to the copper industry, Solomon's ancient "Pittsburgh" has finally been discovered. It was located on the Red Sea. Elath, or Ezion-Geber as it was called in the past, was the naval base of King Solomon as well as a copper refining area at the head of the Gulf of Aqaba. (I Kings 9:26) The huge smelters which have been discovered there are the largest ever found in the Middle East. The ores came from the mines located in the Arabah. The seaport and the copper furnaces and refineries were built by Phoenician technicians who were experienced in such industries.

The present sparse population of this whole area might leave the impression that it was not occupied in biblical times, but actually the ruins of hundreds of villages indicate that at one time this district was thickly settled. Obviously, it could become a very significant territory once again. This has already been intimated by the growth of Elath and the significant role of the Gulf of Aqaba. The territory occupied previously by Edom was roughly 100 miles long and 20 miles wide.

The kingdom of Edom was gradually destroyed, due partly to Assyrian, Babylonian and Persian onslaughts and also to the long struggle with Judah. Jeremiah had predicted that ultimately Edom would be small among the nations and despised among men, and that her cities would be perpetual wastes. (Jer. 49:12-15)

The Nabataeans,* a related tribe, gradually occupied the area and by the fourth century B.C. they dominated the former territory of Edom, as they also controlled that of Moab. Some of the Edomites, pushed out of their own territory, drifted westward across the Arabah and established themselves in southern Judah. Later they became known as Idumaeans.

*The Nabataeans were descendants of the oldest son of Ishmael, and Esau's brother-in-law. Timna became the concubine of the oldest son of Esau and bare Amalek, the progenitor of the Amalekites.

The character of the Edomites was well described in the prophetic blessing which Isaac gave to Esau: "By your sword you shall live." (Gen. 27:40) The heyday of the Edomite kingdom extended from the thirteenth to the eighth century B.C. It was always marked by war and bloodshed. Sentiments such as "Come, let us wipe them out as a nation; let the name of Israel be remembered no more" were frequently heard in the tents of Edom. (Ps. 83:4,5)

Edom is the third nation mentioned along with Moab and the Ammonites in Daniel 11:41. They, too, shall be delivered out of the hand of the Antichrist. It is true that as a nation they may have lost their identity or may have been absorbed by the Nabataeans. Certainly the territory they once occupied is contested today. They, along with Moab and Ammon, are in the area occupied today by the modern kingdom of Jordan.

The Arabs

According to Scripture the Arabs descended from Abraham through Ishmael. God granted a special blessing to Ishmael because of Abraham. Speaking to Hagar, the mother of Ishmael, the angel of the Lord said: "I will so greatly multiply your descendants that they cannot be numbered for multitude."

In response to the plea of Abraham, God said: "As for Ishmael, I have heard you; behold, I will bless him and make him fruitful and multiply him exceedingly; he shall be the father of twelve princes and I will make him a great nation." The angel of the Lord also announced to Hagar that her son "shall be a wild ass of a man, his hand against every man and every man's hand against

him; and he shall dwell over against all his kinsmen."
(Genesis 16:10-12; 17:20)

As to the numerous descendants, it is hardly necessary
to underscore the obvious fulfillment of this prophecy
throughout history. Even today the Arabian peninsula
alone is estimated to contain some 14 million people.
Arabs are scattered across the Middle East. Other peoples have been submerged in historical tides, but in accordance with the prophetic word the Arabs as a people
have greatly multiplied.

It may be a strange blessing to call someone "a wild
man" (A.V.) or more literally "a wild ass of a man."
(R.S.V.) The word literally designates the wild ass, so
called in Hebrew from its running, as it is a very swift
animal. The poetic description of the wild ass in the
book of Job is beautiful:

"Who has let the wild ass go free? Who has loosed
the bonds of the swift ass, to whom I have given the
steppe for his home and the salt land for his dwelling
place? He scorns the tumult of the cities; he hears not
the shouts of the driver. He ranges the mountains as his
pasture, and he searches after every green thing." (Job
29:5-8)

Ishmael and the Arabs are among the families of mankind what the wild ass is among the animals. It is the
image of the free, intractable Bedouin character. The
wild ass is untameable, roaming at will in the desert,
depicting the Bedouin's boundless love of freedom as he
rides in the desert on his camel, hardy and frugal.

The words, "his hand against every man and every
man's hand against him," are a fitting and vivid description of the incessant feuds among themselves and with
their neighbors. It was a characteristic of Esau that he

would live by his sword. (Gen. 27:40) The prophetic description of the Arab character has been confirmed in the innumerable wars among the Arab nations and tribes. Coups and counter-coups are the order of the day.

Recent events furnish an excellent illustration. Saudi Arabia was feuding with Egypt and their armies were confronting each other in Yemen. In 1966 the Syrians accused Jordan of planning aggression against Syria in collusion with the United States and Israel. In 1967 the Arab world was seemingly united against Israel, but disagreements and mutual suspicion could not be overcome.

Time magazine reported that five planeloads of Moroccan troops were grounded in Libya because Egypt had not given them clearance to enter Egyptian air space.[21] The Lebanese army commander in chief, General Emile Bustani, refused an order to open a front on the border of Lebanon, according to an early report, so that Lebanon never did fire a shot at Israeli ground forces during the entire war.

Even after the stunning defeat in June 1967 there was general disagreement among the Arab nations. Calls for summit meetings went out, but the 13 foreign ministers who met in Kuwait were unable to agree on a definite program. At the time, the Arabs were divided on the question of prohibiting oil exports to the United States, Britain, and other western countries. They were also divided on the question of future action against Israel.

That Ishmael "shall dwell over against all his kinsmen" might be said to express a definite geographic location (c.f. 25:18), but there is more in the terms than a mere geographical notice. Ishmael shall dwell inde-

[21]*Time,* June 16, 1967, page 32.

pendently in the presence of all the descendants of Abraham. They have always enjoyed the unimpaired, free possession of the great peninsula from which they have spread over wide districts in North Africa and South Asia to the point that there are over 100 million Arabs today. The ancient prophetic descriptions of the descendants of Ishmael have certainly been justified by history.

Although there is no explicit reference to the Ishmaelites in Egyptian and Assyrian monuments, it is interesting to consider the descendants of Ishmael enumerated in the book of Genesis. (25:13 ff.) Among them we find Kedar, perhaps the most representative. As might be expected, Kedar is associated with Arabia. (Ezekiel 27:21) They are warned by Jeremiah that they will be conquered by Nebuchadnezzar, king of Babylon. (49: 28)[22] Kedar and Arabia are also associated with each other by the prophet Isaiah. (21:13-17)

It is remarkable that the prophets share a deep concern that all nations should join in the worship of God, including Kedar and Arabia. The prophet Isaiah introduced the Servant whom God will uphold, who will bring justice to the nations. This Messianic Servant is given "as a covenant to the people, a light to the nations." (42:6) The great liberation, the unique redemption brought by the Messianic Servant, Jesus Christ, is celebrated. The whole earth is admonished to join in jubilation before the coming of the Mighty Conqueror.

For a long time God had "kept still and restrained himself" (verse 14), but now God has moved into visible action and redemption is assured. The Messianic Servant is a light to the nations and the prophet declares:

[22]c.f. Jer. 25:23 regarding Tema, another tribe descending from Ishmael.

"Sing unto the Lord a new song, and his praise from the end of the earth! Let the deserts and its cities lift up their voice, the villages that Kedar inhabits. . . . Let them give glory to the Lord and declare his praise in the coast lands." (vv. 10-12)

The cities and the villages, the settlements of the oasis, the stationary Arabs and the nomads, all are called to rejoice in God. The bitter enmity and rivalry between the descendants of Isaac and Ishmael have come to an end because all nations are reconciled to God and to each other through Jesus Christ.

It is certainly significant that the Bible, far from breathing a narrow nationalistic spirit, and in spite of the bitter hostilities throughout history between Israel and her neighbors, invites all nations to the worship of God and proclaims salvation for all, specifically for Egypt, the land of Cush, Kedar and Arabia.

Scene 3

God In History

The student of the New Testament should be a historian because the core of the Bible is history. Everything else that the Bible contains is fitted into a historical climax.

"The Bible is primarily a record of events," declared J. Gresham Machen. These words, spoken in 1915, are still relevant. Not only do we find a great deal of history in the so-called historical books, but throughout the prophets, the Psalms and in the apostolic proclamations. Stephen's speech is a review of Jewish history and likewise Paul's address at Antioch.

History has been defined as all that has happened, including everything that undergoes change. This makes history almost all embracing. The history of mankind is a review of all that has happened to mankind. Man has always been anxious to record facts, and ancient inscriptions are the very first attempt in this direction. Herodotus (c. 484-425 B.C.), the "father of history," was followed by many other historians such as Thucydides (c. 460-400 B.C.), Xenophon (c. 434-355 B.C.), Polybius (c. 205-123 B.C.), as well as the Romans' Livy (c. 59 B.C.-A.D. 17) and Tacitus (c. A.D. 55-120).

A significant change occurred with the church father Eusebius (c. A.D. 260-340). He traced all of history back to creation through Israel. This viewpoint dominated from the seventh to the seventeenth century. But history is much more than an enumeration of facts. Obviously, every historian has certain presuppositions. Since he cannot possibly relate all the facts of history, he is compelled to make certain choices, in other words, to impose a viewpoint.

The Greeks assumed that history moved in ever recurring cycles. The first philosophy of history was produced by Augustine (A.D. 354-430), in *The City of God*. He underscored the providence of God, the focus of history in Jesus Christ, and the ultimate purpose of God.

According to Friedrich Hegel, history is the expression of the yearning of man for progress and identification with the deity; history moves toward a goal. Karl Marx saw history as a striving toward the material betterment of mankind, ultimately producing the emergence of a classless society.

Darwin viewed history as a series of evolutions progressing from a lower to a higher achievement. According to the pessimistic outlook of Spengler, decay and doom are inevitable. By way of contrast, H. G. Wells was the apostle of optimism and he wrote: "Can we doubt that presently our race will more than realize our boldest imaginations, that it will achieve unity and peace, that it will live, the children of our blood will live in a world made more splendid and lovely than any palace or garden that we know, going on from strength to strength in an ever-widening circle of adventure and achievement. What man has done, the little triumphs of his present state . . . form but the prelude to the things that man has yet to do." [23]

This was written in 1937, and the outbreak of World War II shattered Wells' easy optimism and in 1945 he wrote: "Homo sapiens, as he has been pleased to call himself, is played out." [24]

Emerson, in his "Essay on Self-Reliance," stated his conviction: "Society never advances. It recedes as fast on one side as it gains on the other. It undergoes continual changes. It is barbarous, it is civilized, it is Christianized, it is rich, it is scientific; but this change is not amelioration. For everything that is given something is taken. Society acquires new arts and loses old instincts."

Arnold Toynbee teaches that history is not determined by race, environment, or blind fate, but is a response to challenge. The challenge may proceed from environment or adversity, from penalization (as in the case of the Jews) or the stimulus of pressures, such as the population explosion. The challenge may be overwhelming, producing arrested civilizations, of which the Eskimos are an excellent example. On the other hand, the challenge may act as a stimulus that is contained and channeled.

This historian foresees that technology "is forcing us all into a kind of socialism. Countries that have a lot of individual liberty are going to lose some if it." Toynbee asserts that "each generation is apt to design its history

[23]*A Short History of the World*, H. G. Wells, page 289.
[24]*Mind At the End of its Tether*, Wells.

of the past in accordance with its own ephemeral scheme of thought." [25]

William McNeill, in *The Rise of the West*, seems to view history as a gradual diffusion of civilization. Karl Jaspers teaches that the philosophy of history in the western world was founded in the Christian faith. God's act of revelation represents the decisive dividing line. According to Jaspers, the axis of history is to be found in the period around 500 B.C., and the spiritual process that occurred between 800 and 200 B.C. During that time China, India, Iran, Greece and Palestine "exploded" spiritually. "Any people that attained no part in the axial period remained 'primitive,' continued to live that unhistorical life which had been going on for tens or even hundreds of thousands of years."[26] Jaspers admits that in the final analysis there is no adequate explanation within the limits of present knowledge for the extraordinary spiritual activity during this time.

The Christian view is distinctly different. The Gospel is good news. It is information about something that has really happened. The Gospel is imbedded in history. This gives a firm foundation to the Christian faith. The Christian knows that God is at work, that he controls all the events of the physical and moral universe, and that he moves toward the fulfillment of his eternal goal. The Christian knows that he is part of this grand design so that his individual life has meaning.

God's concern extends over all nations. "He makes nations great, and he destroys them: he enlarges nations, and leads them away." (Job 12:23) Paul stresses that God himself determined the boundaries of all na-

[25]op. cit., Vol. I, page 193.
[26]*The Origin and Goal of History*, Karl Jaspers, Part I, chap. 1, Yale University Press, New Haven, 1953.

tions. (Acts 17:26) The gracious purpose of God embraces all mankind.

It might be objected that throughout Old Testament history God is basically dealing with only one nation. But it has been indicated previously that God's love was not restricted to one nation. The central fact of the history of Israel is their relationship to God. In this sense their history is a microcosm of the history of all nations.

History has been defined as the "dialogue between God and man-in-pilgrimage in the language of Event; and Christ is the Conversation's middle term, the key to the translation, the light in which the whole pilgrimage can be seen and understood, and the love in which history's brokenness is healed."[27]

Further, says George Buttrick, "The teaching of history is dull because we have turned history into a monologue: man talking to himself. A monologue is always dull after the first few minutes. Soon it makes no sense. Then history becomes a recitation of successive dynasties, a deadly memorizing of kings and dates and battles."[28]

The central truth of Scripture is always Jesus Christ, and his preeminent role is to function as the Redeemer. In this sense, history, according to the Scriptures, is at the same time redeemed and yet not redeemed. It is held in tension, in polarity between two worlds, between the world of men and the mystery of God.

It can be said that history is not yet redeemed because many are blind to Christ and some definitely oppose him. On the other hand, history is redeemed be-

[27]*Christ in History*, George A. Buttrick, Abingdon Press, 1963, page 44.
[28]Ibid. page 91

cause God has spoken the final word through Jesus Christ.

"Once in a public park at Jacksonville, Florida, we heard another spectator of a chess game say of a certain move, 'That's it!' He meant though the other contestant might squirm for a time, even for a long time, that one move had determined the outcome. The rivals might not know the victorious import of that move, and the other spectators might not know, but that particular onlooker knew: 'That's it!' The Bible plays the role of that one perceptive man. By faith, faith being response to the beckoning and grasp of the Mystery, the Bible says of the total Christ Event in history: 'That's it!' God has made a final move in our human story, and his word in Christ 'shall not return unto [Him] void.' "[29]

With Peter, we are looking forward to God's promise of new heavens and a new earth, to the time when the kingdom of the world has become the kingdom of our Lord and of his Christ. Meanwhile, we are assured that Jesus Christ is building his Church, that he is in control of all events, and all the nations are but a drop in the bucket, dust on the scales, and that individually all that happens to us is working for our good if we love God and if we are fitting into his plan. (Rev. 11:15; Isa. 40:15; Matt. 16:18; Rom. 8:28)

Before John describes the apocalyptic judgments which will fall upon the world (Rev. 6-19) he describes a vision of God the Creator in chapter 4 and of Christ the Redeemer in chapter 5. The throne of God is in the center of chapter 4 while the Lamb of God is the symbol of chapter 5.

[29]Ibid. page 27-28

First he presents God as omnipotent, the majestic Creator; next he presents him as Redeemer and the hope of man's salvation. The first chapter underscores the power of God; the next the vision of the love of God. John moves from the first creation to the new creation, and from "believe in God" to "believe also in me."

First of all the absolute sovereignty of God, Creator and Redeemer, is underscored. It is only from that perspective that we can intelligently read the subsequent chapters describing judgments falling upon this world. The Christian can read them without fear because he is assured that at all times God is in control.

John does not furnish actual descriptions of God because he is Spirit, and John can only say that he saw a throne and someone sitting on it. (4:2) At the same time he describes God as the one who is omnipotent and in control—hence the word throne. The burst of light flashing forth from him is as from a glittering diamond or a shining ruby, images of God's holiness and righteousness; the rainbow glowing like an emerald, encircling the throne, is a reminder of God's faithfulness.

When lightning and thunder issue from the throne we are once more reminded of divine power, and the activities of the seven-fold Spirit of God, along with the four living beings, are a fit symbol of the fact that God is immanent in his creation. He is the author of light and life.

At the same time the transcendency of God is perhaps emphasized by the shiny crystal sea spread out before the throne, separating and making the throne unapproachable, a symbol of the remoteness of God. But God is the source of all life and the four living beings are the embodiment of all created life. The doxology is most fitting because all things have been created and called into being by a divine act of will.

In chapter 5 the vision moves from creation to redemption and in the center we find the lion of the tribe of Judah, the root of David, who has conquered and proved himself worthy to open the scroll and to break the seven seals. In the center stands the Lamb whose blood has bought people from every nation as gifts for God. The Lamb is worthy to receive the power, and the riches, and the wisdom, and the strength, and the honor, and the glory and the blessing. This is John's vision, the divine revelation, the necessary preamble before we can face the awesome pictures of judgment in the following chapters.

It is in this very same sense that Jesus, having spoken of the sad condition of Jerusalem and of their captivity among the nations, of the times of the Gentiles culminating in signs in the sun and moon and stars when distress shall characterize the nations and perplexity and fear will predominate, that Jesus said: "Now, when these things begin to take place, look up and raise your heads because your redemption is drawing near."

These words of Jesus are significant. We have no idea how close we may be to the final scene of the last act of the drama of history. The climax may be near. We may perhaps anticipate increasing turmoil in the world, perplexity of nations and distress on a vast scale. No doubt the situation in the Middle East will remain tense, and across the world the political situation will be far from reassuring. Yet it is not difficult to discern God at work.

The final events are impelled by the mystery of lawlessness which is at work and has been at work over centuries. But history under the control of God is progressively moving toward his appointed climax. This is not a time for discouragement but, in obedience to the word of Jesus Christ, a moment to lift up our heads because redemption is near.

Across the pages of history the Church has faced many a crisis. Back in the eighth century the Muslims wiped out Christianity in North Africa and even conquered Spain. The wild Norsemen were threatening from the north and the Magyars were invading from the East. It seemed that very little was left of organized Christianity, not to speak of the evangelical spirit.

The Church has seen times of great trial, but God has promised to build his Church. This is a time to lift up our heads and to recognize the sovereignty of God moving the clock of history. This is the moment to work because it is the day of opportunity. The night comes when no man will be able to work.

Does not the present worldwide turmoil give us ample incentive to proclaim the Gospel? Does not the accomplishment of the prophetic word regarding the restoration of Israel give new assurance and strengthened faith? Shall we not have a renewed vision of Jesus Christ as we lift up our heads? Shall we not have a new understanding of the tremendous need of the masses as we lift up our heads? Shall we not be challenged anew with the task ahead as we consider that the time is short and that Act III may soon come to a climactic end?

With David of old we shall say: "The Lord is my light and my salvation; whom shall I fear? The Lord is the stronghold, the foundation of my life; of whom shall I be afraid." Remember the admonition of the Lord: "When these things begin to take place—look up and raise your heads."